SIMPLE FLY FISHING
TECHNIQUES FOR TENKARA AND ROD & REEL

Yvon Chouinard, Craig Mathews, and Mauro Mazzo
Foreword by Russell Chatham
Paintings by James Prosek

BOOKS®

Ventura, California

One percent of the sales from this book go to the preservation and restoration of the natural environment. In addition, the authors are donating their entire profits from the sales of the first edition to the Native Fish Society, the Atlantic Salmon Federation, and 1% For The Planet. Finally, a portion of the proceeds is being donated to World Trout® Initiative.

FOR THE
PLANET
MEMBER

Simple Fly-Fishing
Techniques for Tenkara and Rod & Reel

Patagonia Books®, an imprint of Patagonia, Inc., publishes a select number of titles on wilderness, wildlife, and outdoor sports that inspire and restore a connection to the natural world.

Copyright 2014 Patagonia Books®
Text © Yvon Chouinard, Craig Mathews, and Mauro Mazzo
Paintings © James Prosek
Paintings on pages 18 to 21 courtesy of James Prosek and Schwartz • Wajahat, New York
Illustrations © Erik Brooks
Photograph copyrights held by the photographers

First Edition

Editor: John Dutton
Photo Editor: Jane Sievert
Design and Production: Monkey C Media

Preserving our environment
Patagonia Books® chose Burgo 100% recycled paper for the pages of this book printed in Hong Kong.

Softcover ISBN 978-1-938340-27-7
Hardcover ISBN 978-1-938340-36-9
E-Book ISBN 978-1-938340-28-4
Library of Congress Control Number 2013957437

Publisher's Cataloging in Publication Data
Chouinard, Yvon, 1938-

Simple fly fishing : techniques for tenkara and rod & reel / Yvon Chouinard, Craig Mathews, and Mauro Mazzo. -- Ventura, Calif. : Patagonia Books, 2014.

p. ; cm.

ISBN: 978-1-938340-27-7 (softcover) ; 978-1-938340-36-9 (hardcover) ; 978-1-938340-28-4 (ebook)
Includes bibliography.
Summary: The best way to catch trout is simply, with a rod and a fly and not much else. Discover where the fish are, at what depth, and what they are feeding on. This book describes the techniques needed to present a fly, make it look lifelike, and hook the fish. Chapters on wet flies, nymphs, and dry flies, the authors employ both the tenkara rod as well as regular fly fishing gear. Paintings by renowned artist James Prosek, technical illustrations, and inspiring photographs and stories throughout.--Publisher.

1. Fly fishing--Handbooks, manuals, etc. 2. Tenkara fly fishing--Handbooks, manuals, etc. 3. Trout fishing--Handbooks, manuals, etc. 4. Fishing tackle. 5. Fishing rods. 6. Fishing lures. I. Mathews, Craig. II. Mazzo, Mauro. III. Title.

SH456 .C56 2014   2013957437

799.12/4--dc23   1404

Contents

PAGE 5   FOREWORD
          Russell Chatham

PAGE 9   INTRODUCTION
          Yvon Chouinard

PAGE 17   CHAPTER 1: TROUT AND THEIR FOOD
          Yvon Chouinard, Craig Mathews, and Mauro Mazzo

PAGE 33   CHAPTER 2: FLY FISHING WITH WET FLIES AND
          STREAMERS
          Yvon Chouinard

PAGE 63   CHAPTER 3: FLY FISHING WITH NYMPHS
          Mauro Mazzo

PAGE 85   CHAPTER 4: FLY FISHING WITH DRY FLIES
          Craig Mathews

PAGE 107 CHAPTER 5: FISHING SITUATIONS
          Yvon Chouinard, Craig Mathews, and Mauro Mazzo

PAGE 141 AFTERWORD
          Yvon Chouinard

PAGE 144 ADDITIONAL RESOURCES

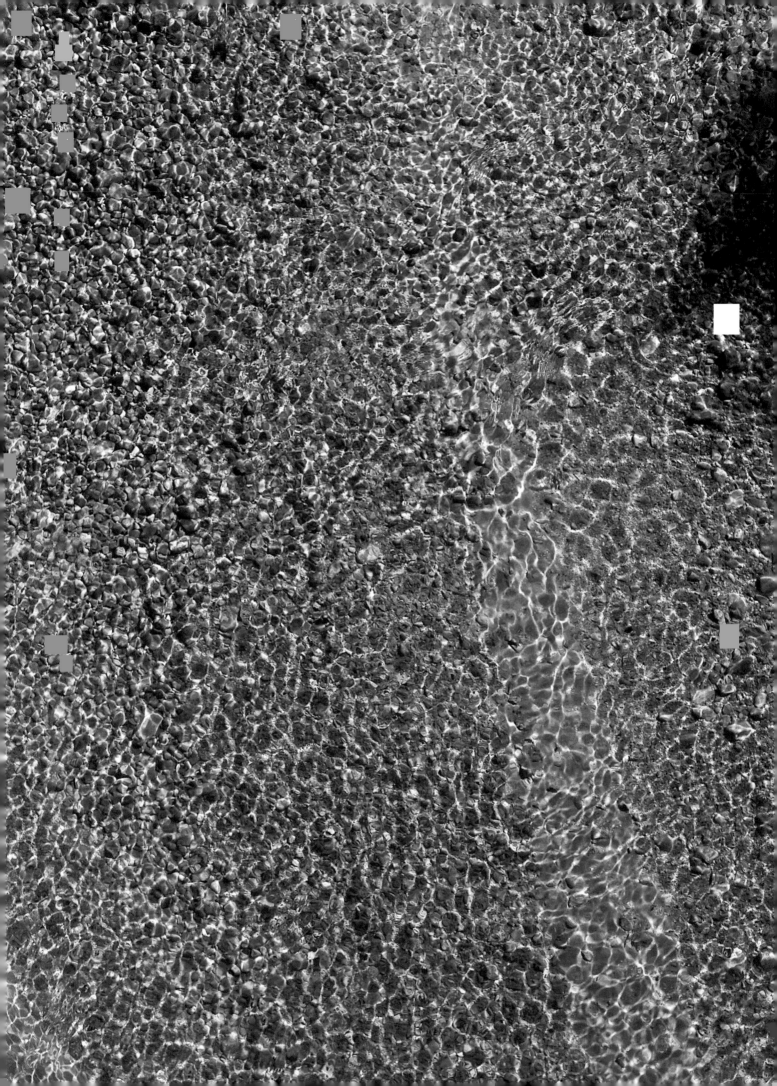

Foreword

The fact is that fishing with an artificial fly has always been an elitist activity. Simply stated, the reason is that at its core lies a set of esthetic precepts rather fundamentally at odds with those of the common man whose approach to life's various aspects is simple practicality. Be that as it may, at the end of the day fishing is still just fishing.

Going back to its origins in Europe, fly casting was practiced in the realm of the aristocracy who owned and controlled the trout and salmon waters appropriate to its use. However, in the literature there sometimes would appear poachers who fell in love with the esoteric essence of this enterprise, and who were willing to risk imprisonment for the sake of its sensual rewards, in one sense a bit like rogering the count's bored wife.

Once transposed to America it became a tad more democratic; but just a tad, as wealthy easterners commandeered private waters in the Catskills and Adirondacks and formed exclusive clubs in New York.

Enter the left coast where many regarded the right as some version of an anthropomorphic museum filled with taxidermied throwbacks, and where fly fishing was mainstream from the start among the great unwashed. In spite of this, it has degenerated into a country club activity popular with the nouveau riche in which the accoutrements have become so ridiculously complex and expensive that Joe Six-Pack can only stand helplessly with his nose pressed to the tackle store window.

One has to wonder how this happened. There are several very simple explanations. The first and most important is that because of our universal environmental crimes, we've ruined most of the fishing close to home: the all-important free fishing that youngsters could readily find after school on foot or by bike.

Because of this, in the late 1970s companies like Fishing International and Frontiers began booking exotic world travel directed at, but not exclusive to, fly fishermen. This changed the angling pastime precipitously. Now, instead of throwing your waders and rod into the trunk of the car and driving for an hour from San Francisco to the Russian River, you wrote a check for a thousand dollars a day to go to Alaska, British Columbia, South America, Iceland, or Russia.

It didn't take the tackle companies long to go on a high-alert point. Suddenly, rods didn't cost twenty-five dollars anymore. Now, instead of plebeian fiberglass, they were made of graphite or boron technology and could set you back four, five, or even six hundred dollars. And the gold- and silver-plated reels that had all the class of a three-dollar whore's earrings were similarly priced. Alright Bucko, if you can afford eight or nine thousand dollars to wet a line for a week, you need the Right Stuff.

It's simple, greed-driven supply-side undemocratic capitalism doing what it does best, which is to demand more and more product and ever-increasing sales. Product lifespan is earmarked at the factory for the flea market, and the manufacturers will handle the public relations on that.

As the great rod designer and builder Tom Morgan has said over and over again, "A good rod is a good rod whether it was made sixty years or sixty days ago." And in this he was echoing the sentiments of every knowledgeable and ethical fine craftsman. But that's not how you sell more rods. First, yesterday's must be categorized as inferior and obsolete. In its place you need some new chemical component with a technical sounding name and a guarantee to make you a better caster. I remember once about thirty years ago being in Dan Bailey's Fly Shop in Livingston, Montana, when a tourist was considering buying a four-hundred-dollar fly rod. The sales associate at the time, Fred Terwilliger, suggested they go out on the train depot lawn across the street and cast it. Pretty soon they were back in the store and Fred said, "Mister, you don't need a four-hundred-dollar rod, you need a fifty-dollar casting lesson."

With respect to fly lines, with the exception of a perfectly level one, which is useless, there are only three basic designs. The most traditional of these is the double taper. Historically, the reason for this was that when all lines were made of silk, you fished half the day with one end, and when it began to sink, you turned it around, greased up the new end and went back to fishing. The weight-forward taper has a heavier section toward the front, designed to fish at greater distances. You false cast this belly, as it's called, then shoot it, pulling the thinner fly line out behind it. A shooting taper, or head, is generally thirty feet long, tied to monofilament, making it the ultimate tool for distance casting. The first two styles, often referred to as whole lines, are generally about ninety to a hundred feet in length. All of these either float, or else sink at varying speeds.

I recall quite clearly in the 1950s when Scientific Anglers introduced the first plastic lines (heretofore, fly lines were woven of silk, nylon, or Dacron fibers). They produced the three aforementioned styles in white, which floated, and dark green, which sank. They worked closely with, and listened to, one time world-record caster, Myron Gregory, who brought to the table all the physical knowledge of the R.L. Winston Rod Company ("Rod Builder to the Champions") and the Golden Gate Angling and Casting Club, both in San Francisco.

A year or so ago, I went through a new Scientific Anglers catalogue. In it were pictured and described about eighty different fly lines. Eighty. It seems that a line good for Florida's west coast is all wrong for its east coast, and of course neither are suitable for the Keys. And the line that's correct for Chesapeake Bay will not do for the Jersey Shore, and of course is also dead wrong for the flats around Nantucket. And don't get the idea that you can transpose your British Columbia steelhead line to Iceland's Atlantic salmon rivers. How naïve can you get? And so on until the minutiae becomes a spinning top whirling to the *kachinging* of the cash register.

The all-time perfect system in distance casting for steelhead and salmon as well as tournament events was developed in San Francisco in the 1940s and perfected in the 1950s. It was simply a thirty-foot shooting head for fishing, and fifty for competition, backed by nylon monofilament. Early on, this material was very hard to handle, being wiry and easily tangled. Eventually however, the Sunset Line and Twine Company in Petaluma, California, developed a brand they called Amnesia that eliminated those problems.

What disturbed the fly line manufacturers to the point of distraction was that this running line cost the user about a nickel a mile so it was systematically denigrated in ads and articles. Soon, an array of more costly substitutes began coming on the market, not one of which ever came close to achieving the perfect efficiency of Amnesia. What this did was cause people to buy thousands of yards of expensive ineffective shooting line, thereby completely destroying the shooting head's real value.

Because of this the stage was set for something new, or rather something old retooled and pressed back into service. It's been some twenty years now, I suppose, since the appearance of the two-handed rod fad. The glamour fish are the sea trout and salmon, and as a general rule, catching them requires a longish cast. To become genuinely proficient at distance casting with a traditional one-handed nine-foot fly rod requires 10,000 hours of practice, and people who can afford to pay eight to fifteen thousand dollars a week to go fishing don't have that kind of time to practice because they're too busy making money.

I learned about double-handed casting from some Scottish gentlemen who visited San Francisco in the 1950s. The rather autoerotic version(s) of Spey casting as now practiced in America would be unrecognizable to these men. I've been everywhere on the planet where you can fish for anadromous fish, and have watched with mild amusement as the captains of industry strained, slashed, and grunted out fishable casts, only to just stand there like designated rod holders devoted to supporting their enormous tackle while the huge lines swung with the current, the owners unable to manipulate the fly—the central act in fishing.

I've seen many times and in many places men and women learning to make fishable casts in a short day. A little whooshing, a little swishing, and with a flourish the fly, probably an absurdly large one, plops down at eighty feet every time. Perfect. Now the good news for the industry: Technology that puts anglers in the bucket comes with a curse involving their checkbooks. Forget six hundred for the advantage of a very long rod, now it's a thousand. And you'll also need a bigger, much more expensive and uglier reel, not to mention a large bag full of specialized fly lines.

Many people, myself included, first learned to fish with a stick of some kind, probably willow, with a piece of line attached to it at the end of which was a hook and a wiggly worm. This ultimately low-tech accessory put the young angler in the closest proximity to the water and the quarry. Wet shoes and pant legs were ubiquitous. Here was the essential undergraduate course that instilled an intimate love of fishing so that no matter what brand of sophistication followed throughout the years, those early memories were etched forever.

So it is: The more complex technology is allowed to intrude upon the fundamental simplicity of fishing, the further one becomes removed from its core value. At its most profound, fishing is a way of remaining forever a child. Of course, we cannot truly do that, nor should we want to, but the illusion of it is one important key to mental health.

All concerned people in this country wish that the upcoming generation would spend more time out in the natural world. There are some conservationists who are opposed to fishing and hunting, but I'm sorry, they are not thinking it through. In order to transpose mere interest into passionate love requires proactive behavior. The road is an uphill one because today's youth of the digital world are raised with offers of passive, instant gratification. Can a person raised in that environment ever fish all day without a bite? Maybe it should be mandatory for schools to provide environmental study from grade one in which there is no computer involved, or any other electronic visual aide, only calm, analytical conversation mixed in with visits to if not wild places at least rural ones.

This brings us around to the tenkara style, a perfect way to eliminate mechanical moving parts, an homage as it were to the willow branch. I'm not a trout fisherman, so my long Japanese rod is used on still waters near where I live in Northern California.

In the fading light of a perfectly quiet evening last November, I was standing by a beautiful pond. To my left, a pair of mallards noodled around the lily pads and red-winged blackbirds trilled their beautiful song, while a bullfrog announced his presence from the tules on my right. My pant legs and shoes were wet and muddy, and as the sun dipped behind the hills I started to shiver. I danced a little fly across the water and six-inch bluegills raced to hit it. Time stood still. I was an eleven-year-old boy again, sneaking concealed along Sleepy Hollow Creek, advancing toward a bay tree root where I knew there were baby steelhead hiding. Mom said not to be late for dinner, but I wasn't hungry. I was as happy as you can get.

Russell Chatham
Marshall, California

*"DESPITE RUMORS TO THE CONTRARY, THE PARAMOUNT OBJECTIVE IS:
TO CATCH FISH . . . ."*

—Sheridan Anderson, *The Curtis Creek Manifesto*

Introduction

YVON CHOUINARD

Why write one more book about fishing when there are probably more books on the subject than romance novels?

Since the fifteenth century, every nuance of fly fishing has been written about in the utmost detail, leaving us to endlessly reinvent what has already been discovered. A tiny change on a classic fly and the "inventor" gets to name it after himself and collect a dime for each one sold. Many of the books on technique are like business books where a minor theory is spread out over three hundred pages, when all it really merits is a magazine article.

Heaven knows we fly fishers are suckers for every new gizmo we think will give us a leg up on catching fish. We wear vests with twenty pockets and waders with even more storage. And as if that isn't enough, we have lanyards, waist packs, and backpacks to carry even more impedimenta. Hundreds of fly lines are now available to us, yet I seriously doubt you will catch one more trout with a line fine-tuned to the conditions than with a classic double taper. The no-nonsense fly fisher Rob Brown, from Terrace, British Columbia, looking over a steelheader's array of fly boxes filled with hundreds of garish flies, said it best when he asked, "When did the green-butt stop working for you?"

I would offer that this proliferation of gear is supported by busy people who lack for nothing in their lives except time. Our "time-saving" communication devices, like tablets and smartphones, make slaves of their owners. We are unwilling, or unable, to put in the 10,000 hours needed to become a master fisher, hunter, or mountain climber. Instead, we load up with all the latest stuff and hire guides to do everything for us—including tying on the fly and releasing the fish. The guides have become enablers rather than teachers. How many bonefish would average anglers catch if they had to work out the tides and wade and spot fish themselves instead of waiting for a guide to bark, "ten o'clock, forty-foot cast now! Wait . . . strip . . . strip"? The guides leave clients so unsure of themselves that they think there must be some secret, unattainable knowledge that only the guide possesses.

As author Sheridan Anderson says in *The Curtis Creek Manifesto*, the objective of fishing is to catch fish, but in the pursuit of the catch you will gain so much more. The higher purpose of practicing a sport such as fly fishing, hunting, or mountain climbing is to affect a spiritual and physical gain. But if the process is compromised, there is no transformation.

Fishing with a fly can be such an incredibly complex and passionate sport that no one can fully master all the different disciplines in one lifetime. Some anglers prefer to limit themselves to only fishing with dry flies, while others specialize in perfecting their casting, fly tying, or even learning the Latin names and life history of all the insects. These can

Opposite: An angler with a "loop rod." Artwork for the first fishing book published (in 1496) in English: *A Treatyse of Fysshynge wyth an Angle*, by Dame Juliana Berners.

be legitimate endeavors in themselves, and there are untold books written about these subjects. This book is not one of them.

This is a book for the young person who wants to learn but feels intimidated by the complexity, elitism, and expense of the sport. He sees his father who owns multiple thousand-dollar rods and reels, fishes only with guides at five hundred plus dollars a day (plus mandatory tips), and flies all over the world to stay at luxury lodges. And the son thinks, "This is not for me."

It is also for the woman and her daughter who are put off by the image of the testosterone-fueled "rip-some-lips," good-old-boy, bass and trout fisherman who has turned the "contemplative pastime" into a competitive combat sport.

This is also a book for the experienced angler who has all the gadgets and gizmos and discovers he or she wants to replace all that stuff with skill, knowledge, and simplicity. It is for the person who believes that a design or a piece of art or a sporting endeavor is finalized and mastered "not when there is nothing more to add, but when there is nothing more to take away," as Antoine de Saint-Exupéry advocated.

It's for the person who thinks maybe it's time to look at the raked Zen sand garden with its three stones and see if he or she can convey the same powerful, evocative image of space and balance with only two rocks or even one.

Most anglers soon discover simple fly fishing helps preserve our capacity for wonder. It can teach us to see, smell, and feel the miracles of stream life—with the beauty of nature and serenity all around—as we pursue wild fish.

Modern-day Balinese fishermen on the southeast coast of Sanur. *Photo: Willem Sorm*

The Day I Learned to Kayak

The Gros Ventre River below Slide Lake falls over one hundred feet per mile, and in the spring runoff has few eddies to pull out and rest in. If you bail out of your boat, you can only hope to find it miles downstream where the current slows as it enters the Snake River.

I had just learned to do an Eskimo roll using only my hands and got a wild hair to run the river solo and without a paddle. A kayak paddle is a powerful tool. You can use it to slow down, speed up, or brace to keep from tipping over. And at the last second, you can do a quick sweep or Duffek stroke to avoid a rock or a suck hole.

Without a paddle, I had to sit low in the boat with my hands in the water. Whenever I went over a steep drop, I had to resist the tendency to lean back. I turned by putting the boat on its side and pressing the nose down just like carving with skis. I had to look far ahead to plan my line. It was pointless to fight the current; I had to let the river tell me where to go. That was the day I really learned to kayak.

– Yvon Chouinard

The Gros Ventre River. *Photo: Kevin Wittig*

THE TENKARA ROD

Many of us of a certain age remember our first fishing pole. We would go to the local sporting goods store and buy a long bamboo pole—what was then called a Calcutta. A line, with a worm or fly on the end, was attached to the tip. For centuries, perhaps even before the time of Christ, this is the way people all over the world learned to fish—and still do.

tied to the tip. The lines, which are about one or one and a half times the length of the rod, are twisted from the tail of a white stallion, starting with fourteen or sixteen hairs and tapering down to three at the tippet end. A short, nylon tippet is added and one to five soft-hackle flies are tied onto the tippet one foot apart. Casting is done using various overhead, roll,

At eighty-three years old, Arturo Pugno, the master, needs no polarized glasses to spot fish. Sesia River, Italy.
Photo: Mauro Mazzo

Twenty-five years ago, a Japanese friend gave me a telescoping fiberglass rod with no reel seat. It was a beautiful, precious gift; light, sensitive, and elegant. When I received this rod, I didn't really understand what I was getting, and I stored it on a shelf in my cabin for fifteen years. I have since learned that it is called a tenkara rod, which means "from the heavens," and is used in Japan to fish for yamame, amago, and iwana trout in small mountain streams.

Some years later, I fished the Sesia River in Italy with Mauro Mazzo. He mentioned that the traditional way to fish the Sesia is to use an eleven- to sixteen-foot-long rod with no reel and just a horsehair line

and Spey casts. It's particularly effective in winter with a size 22 purple-body soft hackle for wary and selective grayling. The hackles, made from the very soft feathers of a bird called ciuffolotto, maintain their lifelike action in the river. There are still about twenty practitioners of this technique in Italy, of which ten make their own lines.

The next summer, Mauro and I decided to try the tenkara rod on a willow-lined meadow creek in the Wyoming Range. It was a very windy day in August, and grasshoppers were being blown about, so we put on a muddler and fished it upstream as a hopper and downstream as a sculpin. The thin, heavy horsehair

Daniela Prestifilippo catches her first fish ever after a few minutes of tenkara lessons with Yvon Chouinard. Cottonwood Creek, Wyoming. *Photo: Mauro Mazzo*

line cut through the wind far better than a floating fly line. Every bend of the creek had a pool, and we moved from pool to pool without having to reel in line and let it out again. We caught fish in every pool: nice cutthroats up to sixteen inches.

Mauro's girlfriend, Daniela, who had never fished a day in her life, picked up the rod and in less than five minutes landed the biggest cutthroat of the day. "Easy," she said. "What's the big deal?"

I think this centuries-old technique was perfect for fly fishing that day and more effective than anything that has come out of our high-tech fly fishing industry. In fact, this is the same gear and technique traditionally used by French and Japanese market fishers. When your living depends on supplying restaurants and hotels with trout, you're not going to waste money on seven-hundred-dollar rods, five-hundred-dollar reels, and three-dollar flies.

Learning to fish with a tenkara rod and a short line is the easiest way to learn to fly-fish. It can be taught to an eight-year-old in minutes. Put her on a riffle

with an old-fashioned soft-hackle fly, and she can outfish dad on the first day. Catching fish right from the start is the way to catch an angler for life. And dad can become a better fisher by applying the lessons learned from this ultimately simple method to fishing with his regular gear.

Other than learning to fish where the fish are, the most important thing an angler can do to catch fish is to control the action of the fly. It's more important than the color or size of the fly, the time of day, or getting off a perfect cast. Why is a worm so effective? Because it is always moving. Why have soft baits replaced hard spoons and lures? Because they bend and flex in enticing ways.

Too many fly fishers are so fixated on launching long casts that they end up putting the fly beyond where the fish are. And with those long casts, they cannot control what the fly is doing.

This is especially true of steelheaders and their long Spey rods: Most steelhead are close to the bank, not in the middle of the river. I once watched the great

After a five-minute lesson, nine-year-old Lola proceeded to land seventeen rainbows in a day and a half. Fall River, Idaho. *Photo: Jeremy Koreski*

steelheader Harry Lemire fish behind a friend of mine. Lemire was walking the bank, making short casts with a floating line and making his signature fly, the Steelhead Caddis, wake, swim, twitch, and flit around on the surface. He was hooking fish just behind my friend who was wading deep, casting long, and not catching anything. Control is everything.

In this book, we use the simplest of all fly fishing methods, a pole with a line on the end, to illustrate how to control the fly without the complexity of modern equipment getting in the way. Getting the fly

to the depth where the fish are feeding and imparting motion to the fly is critical. This is where the tenkara excels. You will catch fish using simple methods and knowledge, in an elegant and artful way. This is fly fishing at its most basic, and like kayaking without a paddle, it brings you closer to the simple truths of the sport. When you pick up (or go back to) a rod and reel, you will be a more complete angler. I believe you will also enjoy your time on the water more and, to Mr. Anderson's point, catch more fish.

Sheridan and I had a contest one day to see who could catch the biggest fish. I won with a twenty-three-inch brown trout. This drawing from him was my "award." – Yvon Chouinard *Drawing by Sheridan Anderson*

Chapter 1: Trout and Their Food

Trout's needs are simple: easily accessible food, cold clear water, and shelter from predators like otters, mink, humans, and many fish-eating birds like ospreys, herons, and pelicans. The various species of trout act somewhat differently from each other. Not only do they occupy different parts of a river, they are active at different times of the day, eat different foods, spawn in different places, and are fooled into taking different artificial flies fished with different techniques. We speak in generalizations here, but it does help to know the usual behavior of your quarry.

Rainbow trout live in the fastest currents, cutthroat trout in quiet eddies behind snags, brook trout in the pools at the inner bends of streams. Marble trout, bull trout, and other char are in the deepest pools. Small brown trout will be in slightly slower water than rainbows, and big brown trout will be in even slower water, tucked into cutbanks or in front of or behind boulders where they can lie in wait to ambush baitfish. Lake trout will cruise the lake edges right after ice-out or in the late fall. At other times, they live in the deep bottom of lakes.

These places are their normal lies where they feel at home and secure. They move to other parts of the river in floodwater, low water, when the water is warm or very cold, when there is a hatch, when they are resting or sleeping, in bright light, low light, and at night.

In high water, fish migrate to the banks to stay out of the fast currents and to take advantage of the worms, beetles, ants, and other terrestrials being swept into the river by the floodwaters. If the water is very dirty, they position themselves right next to the bank, a rock, or the bottom in order to keep their equilibrium. In warm water, they move to the deeper cooler waters or place themselves near a cool spring or tributary. Alternately, they could be under the fastest turbulent cascades where there is more dissolved oxygen.

After hatching, young trout (parr) dart back and forth feeding on plankton, diatoms, and algae. As they become larger, they transition to feeding on insects, which they require for growth. At this stage, when they are less than six to eight inches long, most species of river trout occupy similar territories in the river and display similar behaviors. When they become larger, they begin to occupy their preferred lies in the stream.

When a hatch begins, the trout move from their secure resting lies into more productive water. It can be shallow riffles where the nymphs are emerging or next to foam lines that concentrate and transport food. They jockey around to be first in line without getting their tails nipped by a big boy. The larger, more aggressive fish have the best feeding stations; ideally, these will also be their more or less permanent lies.

Larger trout, sixteen inches and up, begin to exhibit even more different behaviors according to their species. These large fish need to eat more than tiny mayflies. They need the calories afforded by salmonfly nymphs, grasshoppers, crustaceans, baitfish, mice, swallows . . . ducklings. Brown trout transition to feeding on this larger food base sooner than rainbows.

Opposite: Westslope cutthroat and bull trout. Flathead River, Montana. *Photo: Patrick Clayton*

THE QUARRY

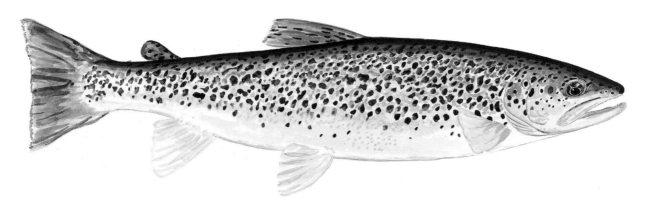

BROWN TROUT

Big brown trout, unlike humans, learn from their past and have a reputation for being smarter than other trout. They are shy, selective, wary, and not easily fooled. Browns like undercuts and overhanging banks and brush, boulders, rock cliffs, and deep pools. They are very hard fighters and often jump when hooked, then take off on bulldogged runs into the depths of the river or lake.

They are most active in low light or at night, when they can leave their secure lies to maraud around the shallows and pools looking for smaller fish. In the middle of a bright day, they become very picky eaters. A dry fly must be perfectly presented and drifted with no drag, and it might take a good emergence of mayflies, caddis, or stoneflies to bring them to the surface.

RAINBOW TROUT

Rainbow trout are the acrobats of the trout world; when hooked they take to the sky. There are several species of rainbows that occupy a wide range of habitat from large, roaring mountain rivers to tiny spring creeks. Rainbow trout are some of the hardest-fighting fish known to freshwater anglers. If rainbow and brown trout are present in the same river, anglers often catch more rainbows because they occupy water more easily fished: riffles, pockets, and pools.

CUTTHROAT TROUT

Cutthroat trout display behavior more like brook trout than their rainbow trout cousins. They are most often found in quiet current tongues along undercut banks, under rock ledges and deadfalls, and in slow, deep pools.

The cutthroat is often easily fooled, and its curiosity about big, bushy flies with bright colors and tinsel is legendary. They like to chase their prey and are suckers for large, rubber-legged dry flies slapped on the water and twitched. They have a reputation for being easy, but during a pale morning dun emergence they can be the most selective feeders, focusing on only one stage of the mayfly.

Cutthroat trout fight stubborn and hard along the bottom of the river or stream. These fish need cold water and prefer solitude, making the best fishing for them a chore, but worth every bit of the effort.

GOLDEN TROUT

The most beautiful of all trout, the golden trout is more than just golden in color; it also has various shades of lavender, pink, blue, yellow, and red.

They live above 10,000 feet in the streams and lakes of California, Alberta, Montana, and Wyoming. In the high-altitude lakes, they have a reputation of being picky eaters, probably because they feed mostly on tiny chironomids (midges).

A marble trout caught on a nymph using monofilament instead of a fly line. Avisio River, Italy. *Photo: Mauro Mazzo*

MARBLE TROUT

Marble trout (and bull trout) are baitfish eaters. The marble trout is the biggest of the trout species and can pass the fifty-pound mark. They live only in Europe on the rivers of the Adriatic Basin. Marble trout are considered an endangered species, and environmental groups in both Italy and Slovenia are making strong efforts to restore their population. They are a very wary fish, and their preferred habitat is deep and fast water. Marble trout feed mainly at night; dawn is the best time to fish for them. Streamers are the first choice, followed by a nymph and a dry fly.

BROOK TROUT

The brook trout is a species of very cold waters in the high country, or mostly northern climes. It is a foolish fish and naïve compared to the brown and rainbow trout. It is a stubborn and strong fighter, and one of the most beautiful fish in the world. Brookies occupy tiny brooks, streams, beaver ponds, and lakes. It has been successfully introduced into the Patagonia region of South America where it occupies large rivers and bocas, and may reach several pounds.

Brook trout are easy to fool, and are found in places on most rivers and streams that are easily reached: big pools, soft riffles, along undercuts, and under overhanging trees. Mostly though, they are found in soft, deep water, tend to feed lower down on the water column, and are less likely to take surface flies.

GRAYLING

Grayling like water with medium to slow current, a gravel bottom, and a depth from one to four feet. They like clean water, but they also like feeding on gray water drainage, as experienced by Yvon when he fished for them in Italy.

Grayling live in schools; when you find one, persist in your efforts because there will be others around. They are mainly bottom feeders and are the main quarry for the Czech nymph technique. But when a hatch starts, they immediately switch to insects on the surface. When fishing them with the dry fly, try to avoid drag as much as possible; graylings are very spooky fish. Fishing them with nymphs is much easier because they are not wary of human presence and you can get quite close. Fish them on a short line to have greater control of your fly.

The Minestrone Hatch

During the 1960s, I spent summers climbing in the high Alps of France and Switzerland. When the weather turned foul, which it often did, we headed south for the sunnier Dolomites of Italy. If the weather followed us, we escaped to the topless beaches and limestone cliffs between Marseille and Cannes.

Driving through Italy, I never dreamed there could be fish in the rivers that tumble from the Alps. How could there be? These rivers were all dammed, diverted, channelized, polluted, and mined for gravel. I thought trout fishing in Italy must have suffered the same fate as hunting. Nearly every Italian male owns a shotgun but is reduced to shooting songbirds on their migration to and from Africa. They are plucked, impaled on a stick, drizzled with olive oil, and end up as uccelli carbon.

Five years ago, I discovered I was wrong about the fishing. The streams of northern Italy flow through limestone, creating an alkaline environment (think San Pellegrino mineral water) that supports abundant insect life. I've found the fishing so good in Piemonte and Lombardia that several times I've had grand slams of rainbows, browns, grayling, marble trout, and marble brown hybrids. Now when I pass through Europe, I include a trip to the pre-Alps of Italy with my friend and rabid fisher Mauro Mazzo. The search is for trout, old Barolos, and the fabulous foods of northern Italy.

Driving through the Valtellina, the villages have sprawled so much that it's tough to tell where one ends and the next begins. One time, stopping to fish the Adda River downstream of the village of Chiuro, I was filled with doubt. Traffic careened along several major highways bordering the river, and houses, hotels, and restaurants lined the banks. Crowds of tourists filled the streets. But we were catching fish—fat, red-finned grayling up to two and a half pounds. I thought the fishing was great, but Mauro promised that about 2 p.m. the fishing would get even better. We moved up to a long pool with a sewer pipe coming in from the village. Promptly at two, gray water poured from the pipe, dishwater from lunches of bresaola, pizzoccheri, cheese dumplings, and polenta. A veritable soup of leftovers.

Tiny red worms crawled out of the bottom muck to feed on the minestrone, and the grayling went nuts feeding on the worms. Mauro gave me a small fly tied with only thick red thread wrapped around the shank. The world's simplest fly?

My tenkara rod stayed bent for the next two hours, until all the dishes were washed and it was time to recharge with an espresso.

—Yvon Chouinard
First appeared in *The Flyfish Journal (issue #4.2)*

Opposite: The Hotel Giardini pool on the Sesia River, Piode, Italy. *Photo: Mauro Mazzo*
A nice grayling caught below the "feeding tube." Adda River, Italy. *Photo: Mauro Mazzo*

THE FOOD

"OTHER THAN KNOWING WHERE THE FISH ARE, IT IS MOST IMPORTANT TO KNOW WHAT THEY ARE LIKELY TO BE EATING."

—The O'Dell Creek Gang

Emerging blue-winged olives (a type of mayfly) land on a reel on the Henry's Fork of the Snake, Idaho.
Photo: John Juracek

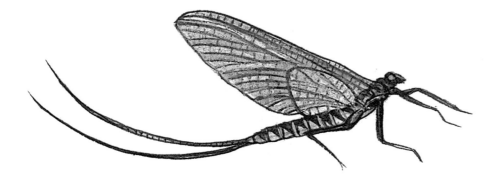

MAYFLIES

Mayflies are perhaps the best-known insects to anglers and are very important in the diet of trout. Mayflies spend all but a few days of their lives underwater and are available to fish all year long.

Emerging mayfly nymphs reach the surface in several ways. Some escape their nymphal skeleton at the bottom of the river or in the water column, with their wings trapping a gas bubble to buoy them to the surface. Others form gas bubbles inside their nymphal shuck that brings them to the surface; still other species migrate to the shoreline to hatch. As a mayfly hatches, it moves and shakes its nymphal shuck in an attempt to escape, causing the shuck edges to shimmer.

The freshly emerged insects are called duns, and even though trout take far more nymph mayflies during the year, there is nothing more visible and dramatic than a trout feeding on duns on the surface.

A day or two later, the insects return to the water to mate and reproduce. They molt and shed their dun skins, becoming sexually mature, and are now called mayfly spinners. Spinners return to the water and lay their eggs, then die on the surface providing one last period when trout can feast on them.

When fishing mayfly hatches, first learn what stage of this insect the trout are feeding on. If mayfly duns are on the water and fish are rising everywhere, first watch the naturals float over rising trout. If trout let the duns pass, the fish are most likely rising to floating nymphs and emergers. If you see trout tails, it is likely nymphs are being taken under the surface. If you see noses, heads, and backs breaking the surface or fish taking the duns as they drift over, the trout are obviously taking duns. If you note casual, unhurried rises with a slow spreading rise ring, then the trout are likely rising to mayfly spinners.

The stage when nymphs hatch into adults, in and under the surface of the water, is when the wet fly works its magic. Fishing a wet fly imitation on the swing—across and downstream—is a deadly technique when fishing for trout taking emerging mayflies.

The most common imitations of mayfly nymphs are Pheasant Tail, Hare's Ear, and March Brown Nymphs. These flies are also excellent searching patterns. If during a hatch you see fish tailing, try these patterns unweighted and fished just under the surface.

Mayfly nymphs are usually fished dead drifted and without motion. A few still-water species are good swimmers, and anglers usually fish imitations with a short strip retrieve.

The best dry fly mayfly emergences are those in which insects are clumsily escaping their nymphal exoskeletons and riding the surface with their nymphal shucks attached. These mayflies trigger good rises of trout because these insects are impaired—trapped in their shucks—and cannot easily escape.

Trout rising to mayfly spinners always rise much more casually and will take spinners in thin water and quiet pools nearer the shoreline. These rises will be quiet takes, merely sips.

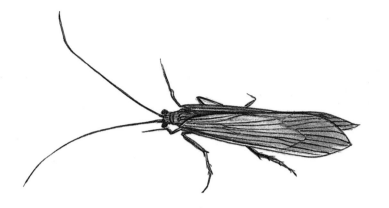

CADDISFLIES

Caddisflies have a three-stage life cycle: larva, pupa, and adult. The transformation from larva to pupa is much like a moth caterpillar spinning a cocoon and later hatching into an adult moth.

Caddis emerge when a gaseous bubble forms inside their pupal skin causing them to shoot from the bottom of the river, lake, or stream toward the surface. They also experience emergence problems as they emerge subsurface and often become entangled in their pupal shuck. Caddis mostly emerge in the afternoon or evening, so by getting close to the rising fish, you can keep track of your cast and the fly as light conditions fail.

Several clues indicate caddis hatches. Early in the hatch, small trout will be seen leaping out of the water as they chase emergers to the surface and their high-speed chases carry them out of the water. There will be no insects on the water since the adults quickly fly off or scuttle to the shoreline grasses. When larger trout rise to caddis emerging in faster currents, you will see bulges or splashes. In slower flows, there will be quiet dimples, slow, porpoise-like rolls, and tails barely breaking the surface.

Caddis pupae are most available to trout when they hatch from pupae to adults. Most swim toward the surface and emerge there, while other species of caddis drift some distance with the currents. In both instances, trout easily capture them, and it is during this time fishing a wet fly or soft hackle on the downstream and across swing is deadly.

Caddis nymph imitations offer a choice between larvae, nymphs, and pupae. Some species of caddis are important to anglers fished as larvae. Larvae are not swimmers, so the pattern is best fished dead drifted near the bottom of the river or stream.

For the larvae, an excellent searching pattern is the Peeping Caddis, which very often is a favorite point fly and deadly for most of the season.

For the nymph imitation, there is the whole family of Czech nymphs patterns, tied on a grub hook weighted on the back to avoid snagging on the bottom, to choose from. They are excellent searching patterns and can be fished any time of the day, in medium to fast water.

At the beginning of a hatch, trout feed on pupae on the bottom, and one of the best flies is the LaFontaine Bead Head Caddis Pupa, fished close to the bottom. As the hatch goes on and pupae come to the surface, it is worth trying to cast an unweighted pupa imitation, such as the LaFontaine Emergent Sparkle Pupa, downstream and let it swing and add a twitch once in a while.

A few caddis species offer good fishing opportunities when females lay their eggs. Look for caddis bouncing on the water, trying to break the surface tension, or for spent caddis on the surface of the water, on boulders, or on your waders. Female caddis might use these as well as overhanging brush and grasses to access the water to lay their eggs.

Rarely will rising trout be selective when taking emerging caddis. But since caddis emergences can be heavy at times, it might seem that your fly can't compete with all the naturals on the water. Here, short, quick, and accurate presentations increase the chances your fly will be taken. A favorite method for taking big trout rising to emerging caddis is to present the fly just upstream of the rising trout, and as the fly approaches the fish give it a jerk with a short pull, causing the fly to be pulled under and then pop up again in front of the rising trout.

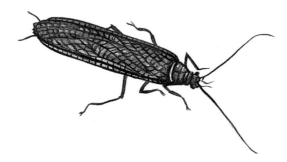

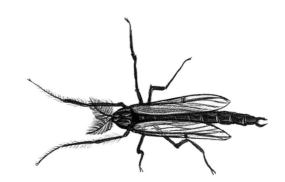

STONEFLIES AND SALMONFLIES

A stonefly's life cycle consists of three stages: egg, nymph, and adult. The majority of a stonefly's life is spent in the nymphal stage (from one to four years); as adults they only live for several weeks. Several days prior to transitioning into adults, the nymphs migrate toward the shoreline to leave the water and emerge.

Stonefly nymphs can be very important to anglers as most species crawl out of the water to emerge. Some stonefly nymphs are quite big, up to one and a half to two inches, and the most common place to fish them are fast-flowing streams. Imitations are very often heavily weighted, and one of the most effective ways to fish them is to cast the heavy fly no more than fifteen feet upstream, let it sink, and follow the drift, first lifting and then lowering the rod tip.

Prime dry fly fishing occurs when female stoneflies return to the water to lay their eggs. Egg laying often occurs in the afternoon and evening hours. There is no doubt when trout are rising to adult stones. Aggressive, swirling, splashy rises can be seen as trout hurl themselves into overhanging brush to chase the adults.

One thing you should keep in mind when fishing dry fly adult stoneflies is flexibility. If a dead-drifted presentation fails, try giving your fly some movement, or pull the dry imitation under and let it pop back up to the surface just upstream of the trout.

MIDGES

Midges are any of a number of small insects. And because midges emerge all year, these tiny insects should be at the top of your list. Midges emerge in the surface film and are susceptible to emergence difficulties, resulting in impaired and crippled adults caught in their shucks and trapped in the surface film. Rises to the naturals are casual and confident as the trout recognize that the insects cannot escape the surface.

The strongest clue to a midge emergence is trout rising when adult midges are skittering on the surface or clustered along the shoreline and no other insects are present.

Trout must expend as little energy as possible when taking tiny insects like midges; they simply cannot afford to use up more calories feeding than what they ingest. Because of this, trout hold just below the surface when taking midges. Here, they will be extremely sensitive to wading waves, and if spooked, they will take longer to resume feeding than if they were feeding on caddis or mayflies.

On rivers, fish midge larvae imitations—the starling and red soft hackle most likely imitates emerging midges—dead drifted in the surface film. When fishing them in lakes or calm-flowing rivers and streams, slowly strip the pupa across the paths of cruising trout. When midge pupae float in the surface film prior to emerging, they swim away from an approaching trout.

A tenkara rod is ideal for winter midging. With no guides or reel to freeze up and fish that do not fight as hard as they do in summer, it is perfect for presenting a fixed-length, pinpoint-accurate cast every time. When we have only an hour or two of daily fishing and each cast can make the difference, tenkara allows the most efficient presentation, as well as hooking, landing, and releasing each trout quickly.

DAMSELFLIES AND DRAGONFLIES

Both damselflies and dragonflies are important to fish and fishers. They thrive in almost all still waters, from large lakes to tiny ponds. Their nymphs are far more important than adults to anglers as they are available all year long in still waters.

Damselfly and dragonfly nymphs crawl out on shore to emerge and expose themselves to trout as they move from their weeded homes to the shoreline to hatch. The nymphs are ineffective swimmers and very vulnerable during these migrations, and trout prey ruthlessly on them. If you see fish quickly dart in knifelike moves at the surface or along the shoreline, they most likely are coming to damselfly nymphs migrating to shore to emerge.

Keep in mind that the nymphs of both insects always migrate in a line perpendicular to the shoreline so imitations must be fished this way, the way trout are accustomed to seeing the naturals. The imitation to use is made with a single marabou feather, in dark green or brown, wrapped around the hook shank to form the tail and the body of the fly. Fish it with a long leader, a few inches under the surface, and retrieve it very slowly.

When trout rise to damselflies, you often see them launch out of the water after the fluttering adults. Adult damsels are available to trout only during mating times or when afternoon winds kick up. When anglers see trout leaping out of the water to chase damsels, this is the clue to try a dry fly imitation.

If the fish ignores your offering, give it a twitch or a short pull on the next presentation. Try twitching or skittering the fly or even pulling it under and letting it pop back up to the surface to sit for a minute.

TERRESTRIALS

Terrestrials is a term that refers to ants, bees, beetles, grasshoppers, and the like. There are no hatches and no nymphs or other stages of aquatic life. Most terrestrial fishing does not involve concentrations of insects as you find when fishing emergences of mayflies or caddis. Sunny, warm, and windy afternoons are always best for grasshoppers, crickets, and mating swarms of flying ants. Beetles and ants also prefer warm, sunny days, but we've had great success using them all year long, even in winter.

Trout rising to flying ants, moths, crickets, bees, and grasshoppers will be noisy and aggressive, whereas rises to beetles and nonwinged ants are subtle, deliberate, and slow.

Flying ant swarms always bring tremendous rises of trout. In late summer, anglers should always be prepared to fish a mating swarm of ants. All trout relish ants and will rise aggressively to them. You will see big trout rising, taking several naturals quickly, like gluttons, before moving on and coming up a few feet beyond.

Terrestrial fishing may require doing whatever it takes—slapping the fly on the water or skittering or waking it on a tight line using drag to move the pattern. Terrestrial fishing does not usually involve heavy concentrations of insects, so anglers must cover more water in search of patrolling trout or cast to undercuts and cover, like overhangs. It is important to remember that trout move distances in search of terrestrials and might be in water where you might not normally expect them to be during other insect activity. Be aware of the water to the rear too.

CRUSTACEANS

Crustaceans include crayfish, scuds, and sow bugs, with the most important among them for the fly angler being scuds. Scuds are the freshwater equivalent of shrimp. They live in any water that has good weed growth and vary in size and color. But like all shrimp, they contribute to the pink-colored flesh of the trout or salmon that feed on them.

If the trout in a particular lake are noted for their pink flesh, that's a good indication of the presence of scuds. If you pull up a clump of weeds, you will probably find lots of crawling and snapping scuds.

They are an important trout food and can easily be imitated by a simple pattern in an olive or tannish pink color. Fish the imitation by letting the weighted fly sink and then bringing it up with small, slow strips.

BAITFISH

Baitfish is a term that includes all the types of fish that are eaten by other fish. These include various kinds of minnows, sculpins, whitefish, suckers, and trout fry and parr. Trout are predators and will even eat the eggs and young of their own species. The largest trout are usually caught with streamers that imitate these baitfish.

LEECHES, EELS, AND LAMPREYS

If we had only one fly to fish with worldwide for trout, salmon, and bass—and even some saltwater fish—it would probably be the olive and black Wooly Bugger. God knows what it imitates, but the way it is normally fished, with slow undulating strips, results in it probably looking like a leech or eel.

Leeches come in a range of colors, including shades of brown, olive, tan, and gray. They swim by elongating and contracting their bodies in a smooth up and down motion. Wooly Buggers are usually weighted at the head to imitate that motion. Wooly Buggers can also be fished very effectively by casting one upstream and letting it dead drift in the current.

MAYFLY LIFECYCLE

CADDISFLY LIFECYCLE

MIDGE LIFECYCLE

APPROPRIATE TECHNIQUES FOR VARIOUS STAGES OF INSECTS

	STAGE	TECHNIQUE
MAYFLIES	nymph	nymphing
	emergers	wet, crippled dry, and dry flies
	duns	dry flies
	spinner	dry flies
STONEFLIES	nymph	nymphing
	adult	dry flies and soft hackles
CADDISFLIES	larva	nymphing
	pupa	nymphing, wet and dry flies
	egg-laying adult	dry flies
DAMSELFLIES/DRAGONFLIES	nymph	nymphing
	adult	dry fly
TERRESTRIALS	all	dry fly
SCUDS	all	nymphing
BAITFISH AND LEECHES	all	streamers and leech imitations

Chapter 2: Fly Fishing with Wet Flies and Streamers

YVON CHOUINARD

I got hooked on fishing at six years of age when my older brother Jeff took me to the polluted (still is) Androscoggin River near our home in Lisbon, Maine. Jeff caught a ten-inch pickerel, secretly put it on my line, and made believe I caught it.

When I was seventeen, climbing in the Teton Mountains of Wyoming, I was watching the mountain guide and excellent dry fly fisher, Glenn Exum, teaching his son Eddie to fly cast. When he saw me watching, he yelled, "Come over here son," and he gave me my first lesson in casting. That was the end of spin fishing with Super Dupers for me.

I've been a serial specialist in every sport I've done. I throw myself into one aspect of the sport, and when I reach 75 percent fluency, I get bored and go on to the next passion. With fly fishing, I started out with wet flies, at first getting tips from my climbing partner Joe Faint who was a Pennsylvania wet fly fisher. Then I moved on to streamers, graduated on to nymphs, and finally got obsessed with "matching the hatch" on difficult spring creeks with tiny flies.

These days I think I'm better balanced; I try to use the appropriate technique for the conditions. Yet I hardly used a dry fly last season. I fished almost exclusively old-school soft hackles. Fifty percent of the time that I fish for trout, I fish with a tenkara rod. I do it not as a novelty, but as a truly effective way to catch fish.

I also fish the salt, but I am not much interested in chasing fish that weigh more than my new granddaughter. I once landed thirty-seven varieties of fish in Indonesia. I hate fishing from drift boats or flat skiffs, and I try to lose the guide whenever I can.

Opposite: Yvon Chouinard executes a circle cast. Fall River, Idaho. *Photo: Jeremy Koreski*

FISHING WITH WET FLIES

Wet flies imitate either baitfish, leeches, swimming nymphs, or emerging caddis and mayflies. The crawling or dislodged and drifting nymphs and scuds are covered in the chapter on nymphing. Baitfish and leeches are in the section on streamers.

For catching sheer numbers of fish, the most effective technique imitates nymphs either dead drifting or swimming to the surface. This chapter deals with the nymphs that are emerging—swimming to the surface to hatch as duns and then adults.

A sixteen-inch trout is not going to get many calories from a tiny size 18 mayfly. There is a net gain of calories only if the effort requires less calories burned than is gained through the food. It doesn't pay for a fish to swim up from four feet down to nab a tiny fly on the surface, especially when there is a good chance the fly will have dried its wings and flown off before it gets there.

Trout are masters at putting out the least amount of energy to gather their food. When they are feeding on small insects, they need a large quantity (a hatch) to make it worth their while, and they position themselves so they expend the least amount of energy to take advantage of that hatch.

The surest deal for them is to intercept the drifting nymphs or the swimming nymphs that are going to the surface or are just under the surface as they are breaking out of their shucks. Another easy meal is crippled flies that are unable to fully emerge from their shucks. Dead adult spinner mayflies splayed out on the surface are also an easy meal.

Trout, of course, feed most actively during a hatch but can be enticed to fall for an artificial fly at any time if the fly can be presented with an enticing action close enough to its lie so it only has to move a little and open its mouth.

The technique described here deals with mostly imitating that emerger stage of the hatch. It is one of the oldest techniques of fly fishing but one that has lost popularity to the dry fly, streamer, and nymph. Yet it remains one of the most effective techniques for catching fish during nonhatch periods. The method

What a fish sees. *Photo: Matt Stoecker*

was very simply described by James Leisenring in his book *The Art of Tying the Wet Fly and Fishing the Flymph*.

I always fish my fly so that it becomes deadly at the point where the trout is most likely to take his food, which is usually at or close to his position in the stream. Since my flies are tied to act lifelike and look lifelike, I fish them so that the efficiency of the qualities is at its highest when it nears and arrives before the trout for his inspection. This is accomplished by allowing a gradual increase in tension caused by the water flowing against the leader, causing the fly to lift from the bottom and rise with the hackles or legs quivering after the manner of the natural fly.

We begin by describing wet fly fishing with a tenkara rod. Not only is it the easiest way to learn to fly fish, but it is possibly the most effective way to catch large numbers of fish.

TENKARA WET FLY GEAR

TENKARA WET FLY RODS

Tenkara rods, now made of carbon fiber and telescoping, are mostly made in Asia. In Japan alone, there are hundreds of models for fishing everything from six-inch smelt to salmon and sea bass.

For trout fishing in Europe, New Zealand, and the Americas, we haven't found an advantage to using a rod longer than eleven and a half feet. The rod should be a bit stouter than the very light and limber rods popular in Japan for fishing very small mountain trout. My favorite is a ten-and-a-half-foot soft-hackle model from Temple Fork Outfitters (www.tforods.com). They also make an eight-and-a-half-foot model for small creeks and an eleven-and-a-half-foot rod for delicate dry fly fishing.

These rods have a two-inch length of braided line glued to the tip called the lillian. Tie a stopper knot in this if there isn't one. To extend the rod, work from the tip toward the butt. Grab the tip near the lilian with your left thumb and forefinger and hold the next section firmly with your right thumb and forefinger. Pull gently until the tip is fully extended and starts to pull the next section through your right hand. Repeat the process with each section until the rod is completely extended. To collapse the rod, work from the butt toward the tip. Start with your right hand near the top of the butt section and your left at the top of the next section of narrower diameter. Push your hands together and repeat until the rod is fully collapsed.

If there isn't a line holder on your tenkara rod, you can easily make one using two pieces of wire bent in a sort of U shape. The easiest way to make these is to use large paper clips and attach them to the rod with rubber bands.

Tie one paper clip on about an inch up from the butt of the handle and another an inch below the top

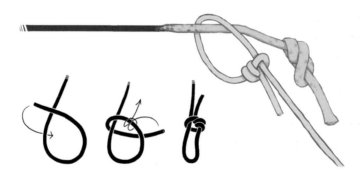

Rod tip, lilian, and stopper knot

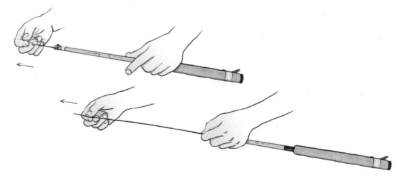

Extending the rod

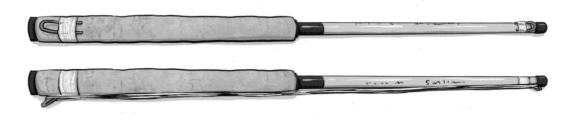

Tenkara rod with line holder

of the first section. You can use string or just rubber bands to hold the wire loops. The fly can be stuck in the cork when walking from spot to spot on the river. I also keep a rubber band on the rod handle to tuck the fly and tippet under.

TENKARA WET FLY LINES

Line choice depends on whether you are fishing nymphs, dry flies, or wet flies and streamers. For fishing wet flies and streamers, I prefer to use a light floating line for my ten-and-a-half-foot rod. The floating line casts better in the wind than monofilament or furled lines and can handle heavier streamers. Since the line floats, it's easier to pick up and mend the line to control the speed and direction of the drift. Also having the line float is an asset in controlling the fly so it acts like an emerging nymph. However, even the lightest floating line may be too heavy to cast well on the more delicate tenkara rods.

You may be able to find a specific floating line for the tenkara rod. If you can't, don't worry as the lines are so short they do not need to be tapered. You have several choices. The easiest and cheapest way is to make your lines by cutting off the back end of an old weight-forward trout line, three weight or smaller. Or find a spool of running line that measures between .025 and .030 inches in diameter. Cortland (www.cortlandline.com) makes a forty-foot level line specifically for the Temple Fork rods.

For a ten-and-a-half-foot to eleven-and-a-half-foot rod, use a twenty-foot length for normal wet fly fishing and a twelve-foot length for small creeks or for nymphing. Also cut an eight-foot section to be used as an extender. The eight-and-a-half-foot Temple Fork Outfitters cutthroat rod can handle a .026 inch diameter line with a length of fifteen to twenty feet.

On the butt end of the lines tie a turle knot, leaving a one-inch long tag. Don't overtighten. Hitch the loop over the lillian and snug it down. The tag is for loosening the knot to take the line off the lillian. On the leader end, tie on a small loop (if there isn't one) using a nail knot, or tie a perfection loop.

TENKARA WET FLY LEADERS

I prefer to tie my own leaders partly because I don't like to spend four or five dollars for five cents worth of nylon, but also because with a knotted leader you can use the knots to tie on multiple flies. The knots also create friction that helps to pull the line tight in the moving water so you maintain direct control over the fly.

EIGHT- TO NINE-FOOT TENKARA WET FLY LEADER

This is the leader for swinging wet flies with the floating line. Tie a perfection loop on the butt of the leader, and tie together the sections listed below with a blood knot or surgeons knot. Hitch the leader loop onto the line loop.

- 15 in. - .017 (20 lb. test) Maxima Ultragreen nylon
- 15 in. - .015 (15 lb. test) Maxima Ultragreen nylon
- 15 in. - .013 (12 lb. test) Maxima Ultragreen nylon
- 15 in. - .012 (10 lb. test) Maxima Ultragreen nylon
- 15 in. - .010 (8 lb. test) Maxima Ultragreen nylon
- 24 in. - .007 4X (6.5 lb. test) tippet material

Hilary Hutcheson on the Middle Fork of the Flathead, Montana. *Photo: Lee Cohen*

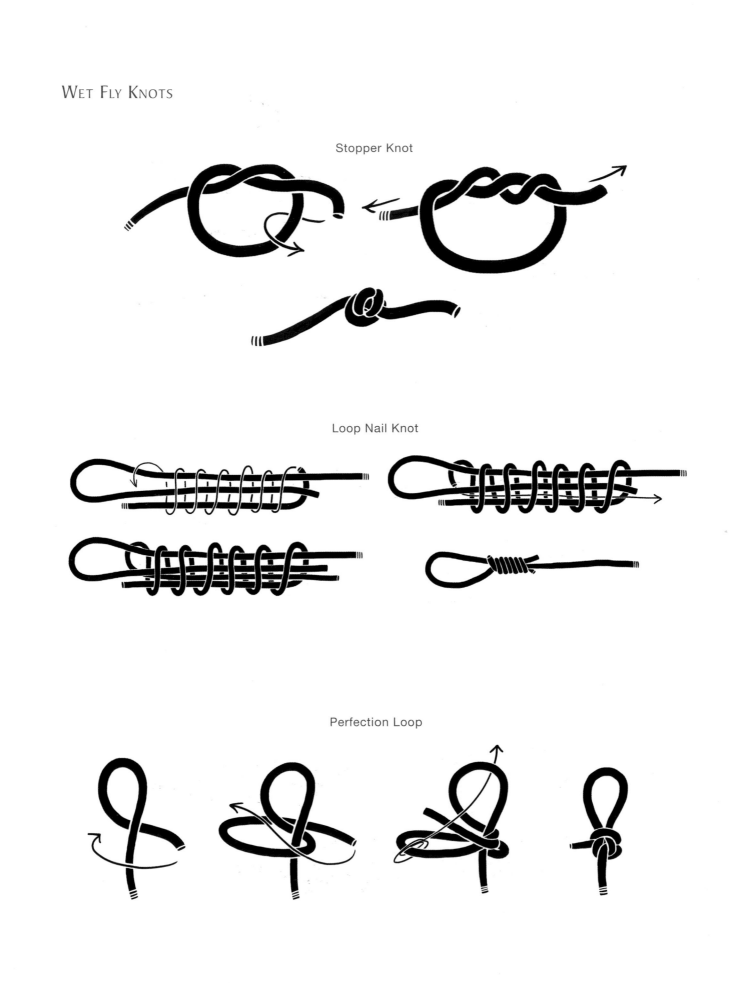

Stopper Knot

Loop Nail Knot

Perfection Loop

Double Surgeons Knot

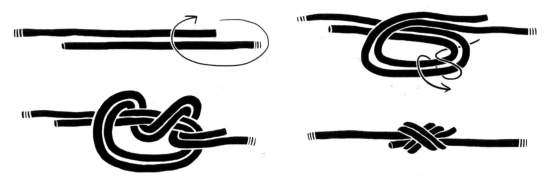

Blood Knot

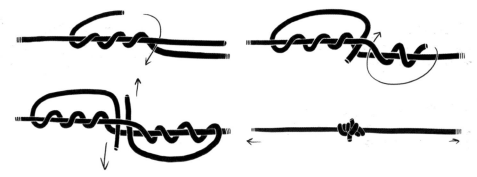

Nonslip Loop Knot

Yvon Chouinard searches for the perfect fly. *Photo: Mauro Mazzo*
Opposite: Washing day in Bhutan. *Photo: Yvon Chouinard*

Bhutan Brown Trout: Here Be Caddis

In 1985, I was in Bhutan to climb Ganghan Puensum, then the highest unclimbed mountain on the planet. Our worthless Chinese and Indian military maps put us on the wrong side of the mountain, so we gave up and settled for making first ascents on some unauthorized 20,000-footers. We corrected the flawed maps and planned to tell our sponsors (National Geographic and Rolex) about our corrections. But standing around the campfire one day, we decided to burn our notes instead. There need to be a few places left on this crowded planet where "here be dragons" still defines the unknown regions of maps. Then I went fishing.

I knew that King Jigme Wangchuck was a fly fisher who had some spring creeks to himself, where he avoided wading by casting from atop an elephant. He was also married to two beautiful sisters and loved playing basketball. We watched a game in the capital city of Thimphu one day. The king waited under the basket (kings don't run) until the game came to him. When he scored, both sides cheered. It's good to be king in Bhutan.

Many of the rivers in Bhutan run clear and cold, and brown trout, introduced by the British, thrive there. Being at the same latitude as Miami, the insect life is prodigious. Some of the caddis cases I saw looked like small cigars.

Fishing near a small village one day, I was ignored by the women washing clothes along the bank next to me. Until I landed a pretty big brown. When I released the fish, the women began screaming, pounding me on the back, and indicating with fingers pointed at their mouths and bellies that they wanted to eat that fish. Their religion wouldn't allow them to kill the fish themselves, but if I killed it . . .

On another river, just outside Thimphu, the air reverberated with a deep Ohmmmmm coming from hundreds of chanting monks in the monastery nearby. I wasn't having much luck, so I sat on the bank, taking in the chants and searching my fly box for answers. I looked up to see a tall monk walking toward me. My gut cramped with fear. You are not allowed to fish within a mile of a temple, or monastery, in this strict Buddhist country, so I recognized trouble.

As the monk drew closer, I imagined myself being strung up in a dark dungeon of some sixteenth-century building. When he reached down and grabbed my fly box, I thought maybe I'd get by with just having my gear confiscated. Then he reached into the box, picked out a large gray nymph, and handed it to me. On the first cast, I hooked a fat twelve-inch brown and released it. The monk clapped and laughed from deep in his belly, just like the Dalai Lama.

—Yvon Chouinard
First appeared in *The Drake*, Spring 2012

CASTING THE TENKARA ROD

THE BELGIAN CAST

The casting techniques are the same as casting a rod and reel, but it is much easier with a tenkara rod because the line is short, the rod is light, and you can keep your noncasting hand in your pocket.

I asked the great fishing icon and caster Lefty Kreh if he could describe how to cast a fly rod in just two sentences. He answered, "Easy, just do the forward cast as if you're throwing a spear. The back cast you throw the line behind you like you're throwing a Frisbee." To do that, you have to stand a bit sideways to the target.

All the rules of normal casting apply. Don't bend the wrist. Keep the rod tilted at a thirty-five degree angle to the vertical on the back cast and ten degrees on the forward cast. Use the core of the body for power like in tennis, throwing a baseball, or kayaking. The line travel makes a small oval in constant tension; there are no abrupt stops. This cast is sometimes called the Belgian cast.

THE SNAP C CAST

This is a change-of-direction cast when there is no room behind you to back cast.

Place the rod parallel with the water with the taught line ninety degrees downstream. Draw a big C in the air with the rod tip, starting at the top of the C, and return it to the start position at the bottom of the C. Now the line is in the water, upstream of you.

Raise the tip to a vertical position. Go back slowly with your hand until the fly line is lying in the water close to your legs. Now start a forward cast like a regular overhead cast. Slowly punch it out.

THE BOW AND ARROW CAST

This cast is done when there is no room to do any other cast. Use the shorter line that is slightly longer than the rod. Reach out and grab the end of the line with your nonrod hand and then grab the fly with two fingers. With the rod close to your body in front of you, point the rod at the target and pull the end of your line and the fly back to your ear, and let go.

Back Cast

Forward Cast

The Belgian Cast

The Snap-C Cast

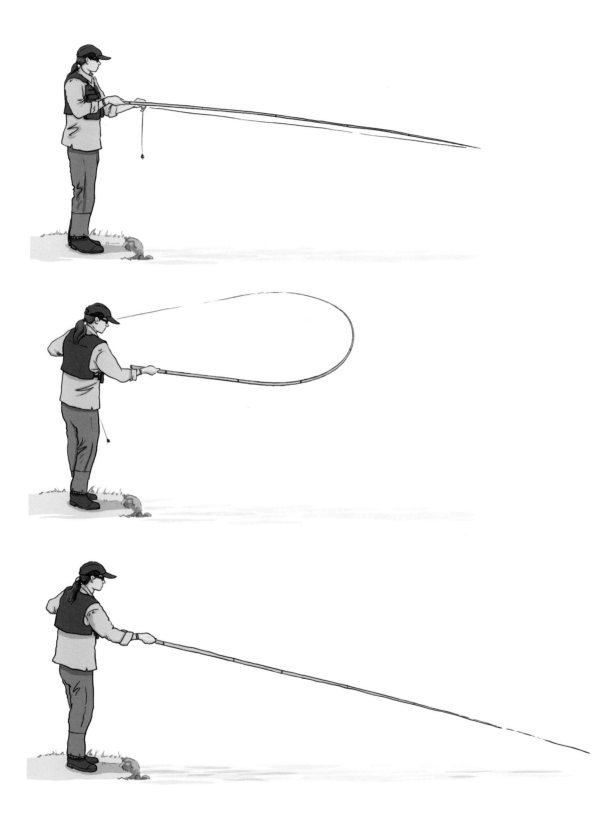

The Bow and Arrow Cast

FISHING WET FLIES WITH A TENKARA ROD

Start by tying a size 14 soft-hackle wet fly onto the end of the tippet using a nonslip loop knot (page 39) or a clinch knot.

Straighten your line and leader so there are no kinks or coils. This is important, as you don't want any slack in your system. I use a small piece of bicycle inner tube to do this by running the taught line through a tightly held fold in the inner tube.

Go to a riffle part of the stream where the water is from one-and-half- to three-feet deep with a current that's not too slow or too fast. Cast the line at about a fotry-five-degree angle downstream. As soon as the fly is in the water lift the loose part of your line and place it across from you.

This mending upstream slows down the drift of the fly. Make sure you don't overmend and pull the fly out of the water. By mending upstream, you are trying to avoid the loose line getting caught by the current and swinging your fly across the current at an unnaturally fast speed.

With your rod at about a twenty-degree angle to the water, follow the line with the tip of the rod. As the line tightens, lift the rod tip up to about a thirty-five-degree angle. As soon as the line comes tight, make an occasional twitch with the tip of the rod. It is important that the tip of the rod moves only two or three inches at most, no more.

To do this, hold the rod with your thumb on the top of the handle and your upper arm held straight down in a totally relaxed position (easy on the rotator cuff). The twitch is imparted to the tip by squeezing the bottom fingers of the hand, not by raising the rod.

If you look at your hand while you are doing this, you hardly see any movement at all. Almost everyone who tries to do this twitch overdoes it at first. Here's the rule: If you think you're not moving the fly enough, move it less. The key is to work only the top foot and a half of the rod. The rod itself hardly moves.

What you are trying to do is imitate the emerging and swimming stages of the caddis or mayfly. This is the stage where they are most vulnerable to a trout. As a result of the twitching action, the soft-hackle fly is going up in tiny increments of one to three inches. It is quite different from swinging traditional wet flies across a current.

In the seventeenth century, this subtle action of the tip was considered so important that the poles were made with a different, more flexible, wood, or even ivory, for the last foot or eighteen inches of the rod.

With a good tenkara rod and the proper tip flex, you have such a direct control of the fly that you can make a caddis dry fly hop around on the water. Trout, steelhead, and salmon do not prefer to attack dead-drifted wet flies and nymphs. Just like a house cat or a grizzly—any predator for that matter—they want action. They want the type of action that imitates emergers, diving caddis, swimming nymphs, or wounded minnows. The best way to imitate that type of action—and to trigger a response—is to use a tenkara rod with a delicate tip and a tight, light line.

Most of the time, a fish will take the fly right after a twitch, whether you are using a waking fly for steelhead, a wet fly for salmon, or an egg-laying caddis for trout.

After each cast, take two steps downstream and cast again. Use the tension of the water against your line and fly to load the rod. One back cast and your line is back in the water. Do not false cast unless it is necessary.

When there are obstructions like trees or a cliff behind you, do a roll cast or a Spey-style cast like a circle C or double Spey to change direction and get the line out. Another advantage of the floating line is it is easier to do these casts, especially if there is a wind.

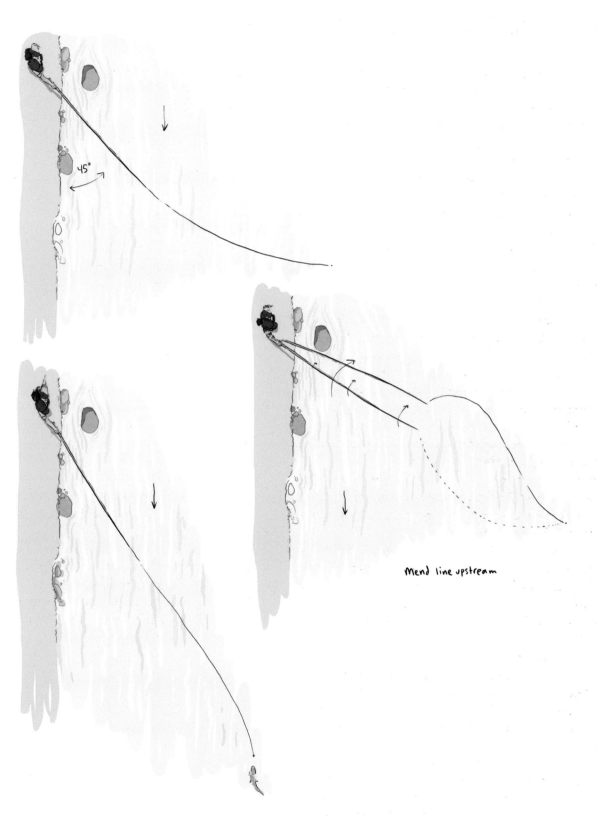

45°

mend line upstream

Wet Fly Fishing Technique

Landing a Fish

When you hook a fish on tenkara gear with this tight-line method, the take is often violent. All that stands between you and the prize is the line and that long, flexible rod. For most trout, you keep the tip up and fight the fish using the flex of the rod. Connect with a bigger, hotter fish, though, and you'd better start running. When your only drag system is your feet, wearing good wading boots is critical. In extreme cases, you can always throw your rod in, strip off your clothes and swim after it like Eddy, the fishing goddess in *The River Why*. The trout will swim away downstream, and feeling the pull of the rod gone, the trout will turn back upstream and head for its lie. The rod will swing downstream of the fish and tire it out. It may take a while, but good things come to those who wait. Often, you can grab your rod handle as it travels past, trailing after the fish.

After a fish is ready to come in, raise the rod up until you can grab the line with your free hand and haul it in hand over hand. Sometimes a big fish in heavy water just doesn't allow you to grab the line. In that case, collapse the rod (from the butt section) until you can grab the line.

Most of the time, you won't need a landing net if you fish a barbless hook. When you get the fish within reach, take your forceps and clamp them onto the hook and work it free of the fish. Avoid touching a trout, but if you need to, grab the lower lip with thumb and first finger and release it via the forceps.

Craig Mathews thankful that he didn't have to take a swim. A not-to-be-named creek in Yellowstone country, Montana.
Photo: Tim Bozorth

Advanced Tenkara Wet Fly Techniques

I generally fish the wet fly method using two flies. I consider this an advanced technique because unless you have the casting perfected you will end up with a horribly tangled leader. With two wet flies, and especially casting two weighted nymphs, if you back cast and forward cast with the line in the same plane, you will end up with a mess. It is important that you have the Belgian cast perfected.

The two-fly method not only gives the fish a choice of flies, but the two flies add more drag, thus helping to straighten the line and giving more direct control of the flies. However, the primary advantage of using two flies is that the point fly and the dropper will have different actions.

To tie on one or more dropper flies, leave a six-inch or longer tag on your leader knots. Make sure the tag is the heavier of the two sections that are tied together, and this will keep the mono from wrapping around itself. Tie the dropper fly directly to the tag.

Another option—the best system I've found to keep the dropper out from the leader—is to stiffen the first two and a half inches of the dropper by doubling it. Tie a loop with a double surgeon's knot and then tie another double surgeon's knot about halfway to the end of the loop. Then hitch the loop above the tippet knot. The double nylon of the loop keeps the dropper away from the leader and can be replaced as the leader gets shorter. This is called the speed dropper by some.

A typical two-fly setup consists of a point fly that should be the heavier or bushier of the flies. This is to add further drag to the line. Think of the point fly

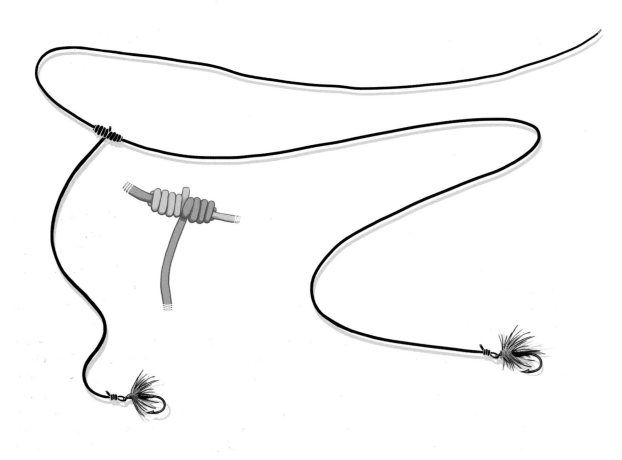

Tag method of tying on two flies

50

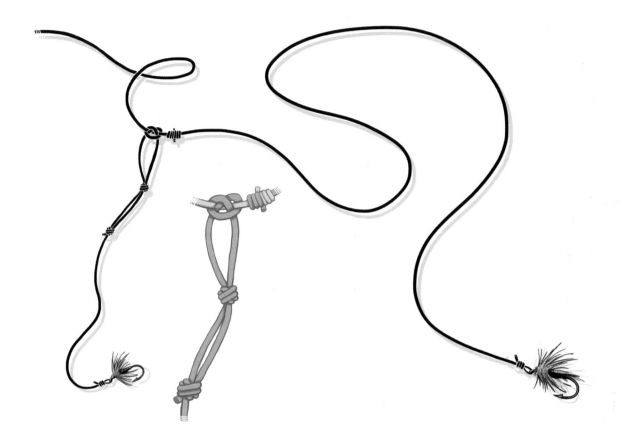

Dropper loop method of tying on two flies

as being an anchor that helps straighten the line after the cast. A typical point fly would be a size 14 soft hackle tied on a 2X heavy-nymph hook and on 3X or 4X tippet, with a smaller or lighter fly for the dropper on 3X tippet. The point fly can be from three to four feet from the dropper.

You rarely have to use lighter tippet, because you're fishing downstream and the leader is not going over the fish. On spring creeks when the fish are wary and the hatches require small flies, you can drop down on your tippet sizing, but be warned you might get the line tangled, especially if there is a wind.

You fish two flies the same way you fish one: twitching and doing a lift at the end of the drift. Periodically, check your leader to see that you don't

have a tangle or wind knot. A wind knot will reduce the strength of your tippet by 50 percent.

If you wish to sink the flies, use a smaller diameter tippet like 5X or 6X and cast farther upstream with slack in the line. If there is fast current, throw a mend upstream to avoid the swing. If there is a slow current between you and the fly, do a downstream mend. When the line is straight downstream, you can twitch the flies and slowly lift the rod up. Don't be in a hurry to cast again. Leave the fly gently swinging on the surface for a few seconds. Think about teasing the fish. You will be surprised by how many times you can induce a take. If you wish to get down really deep, use a tungsten bead head soft hackle for the point fly.

If there are egg-laying caddisflies about, the advantages of a long tenkara rod and multiple flies can really be maximized. Start with a shorter line of twelve to fifteen feet. Extend the distance between the point fly and dropper to four to five feet. Put a Hare's Ear or Pheasant Tail soft hackle on the point, a fly that most resembles the caddis. On the dropper, tie on a dry caddis like an Elk Hair or Stimulator.

Cast upstream, across, or forty-five degrees downstream. At the end of the swing, lift the rod up until the dry caddis comes off the surface a few inches. Make the dry fly hop and skitter on the surface imitating a female caddis trying to break through the surface tension of the water to lay its eggs on the bottom.

The trick to doing these little hops is extending the distance between the point fly and the dropper, and manipulating the last foot of the rod tip. Describing how to do it is like describing how to crack a safe. Just practice and you will figure it out.

You will know when you are properly fishing two flies. You will be hooking fish almost equally between the point and the dropper.

Things get really interesting when you hook two fish at once, which happens more frequently than you might think. For some reason, doubles are usually a brown and a rainbow. Browns are Republicans and rainbows are Democrats, and they never pull together. If they did, you would have a rodeo on your hands.

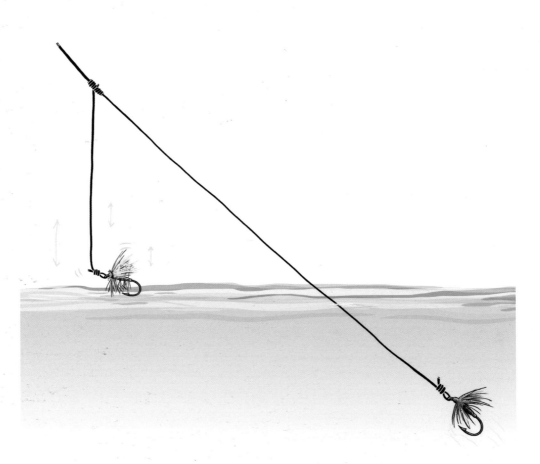

Hopping a dry fly on the surface using an anchor fly

A Quick Study

I took a friend who had never fished before to a stream in Yellowstone where there were lots of aggressive pre-spawning browns throughout the riffles. I gave him my tenkara and a size 8 Shakey Beeley soft hackle. After a five-minute casting, twitching, and landing lesson, I left him alone. Since I had a regular rod, I fished behind him throwing long casts, covering a lot more water than he could with his twenty-foot line. At the end of the day, he caught more fish than I did, including a twenty-four-inch brown that slipped the hook right at his feet.

—Yvon Chouinard

A Madison River brown trout dresses in its autumn spawning colors. Wyoming. *Photo: John Juracek*

MAKING THE LINE LONGER OR SHORTER

Some tenkara rods made for larger US rivers are made stouter than the typical Japanese rods and they can handle lines up to thirty feet. To make a twenty-eight-foot line put a turle knot on one end of your eight-foot extender (that you cut earlier from the fly line) and a stopper knot on the other. Hitch the extender onto the lillian then attach the twenty-foot line above the stopper knot of the extender.

In a pinch you can shorten the line by tying a sheepshank knot. I first tried this on a small mountain stream in Montana. The fish were all concentrated in deep holes under log jams and cut banks and wouldn't come up for soft hackles or dries. I had on a twenty-foot line, which was too long for this creek and too long for short-line nymphing. I shortened the line to ten feet—so only the leader was in the water—using a modification of a sheepshank knot. I put on a heavy bead head nymph and proceeded to catch one to three rainbows from each pool.

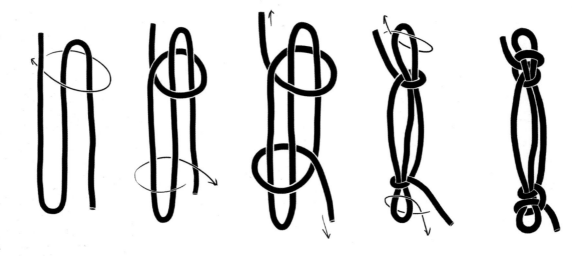

Modified Sheepshank Knot

Line Sag

WET FLY FISHING WITH ROD AND REEL

You can somewhat adapt the tenkara wet fly method to a regular fly rod, but only if you use a long slower-action rod. I recommend a ten-foot two-weight rod and underline it with one-weight line to avoid line sag. You cannot impart action to the fly if there is a sag or slack in the line, or if the line is being blown about by the wind. If you try to do the twitch with a fast action rod you will invariably over-twitch as the whole rod will rise up. Keep your casts short, no more than twenty feet, so you can better control the flies.

Press the line under your finger and just make believe you don't have a reel. Unless you hook a big fish, don't use the reel, just haul the fish in like you would on a tenkara rod.

In this kind of water there can be fish holding almost everywhere. Eliza Clayton fishes for western cutthroat on the North Fork of the Blackfoot River, Montana. *Photo: Noah Clayton*

WET FLIES

I have replaced all my traditional winged wet flies with soft-hackle flies. Since there is no top or bottom to the fly, there is never a worry that the fly is swinging on its side or upside down. I'll use a winged wet fly only if it is meant to imitate small baitfish rather than an insect.

Properly tied soft-hackle flies are almost impossible to find in most fly shops, but they are simple to tie, and I strongly recommend that you learn to tie your own.

I tie my flies with one important difference from traditional soft hackles: I tie most of them with a thorax made of Hare's Ear Ice Dubbin. This is hare's ear fur plus a bit of synthetic glitter. This has two advantages. The thorax, which is tied after the hackle, keeps the hackles open so they don't lie against the body, and the sparkle in the dubbing when wet, looks like the air bubble of an emerging nymph. It's similar to what a gold bead does to a nymph pattern.

SOME ESSENTIAL WET FLY PATTERNS

Partridge and Pheasant Tail

In smaller sizes, this fly imitates the nymph or emerger stage of almost every mayfly; in larger sizes, it serves to imitate caddisflies or stoneflies. If I were to limit myself to only one soft-hackle pattern, it would be this one in size 14.

Hook: #12 to #18, Dai-Riki #075 nymph, 2X strong, 1X short

Thread: 8/0 brown

Tail: pheasant tail or brown Zelon on smaller sizes to imitate the shuck

Body: pheasant tail

Ribbing: extra-small copper wire

Thorax: Hare's Ice Dubbin peacock blend. To imitate a pale morning dun emerger, I use the lighter color Hare's Ice Dubbin hare's ear blend.

Hackle: partridge

Mormon Girl

This pattern is a good imitation of the yellow sally (Mormon girl) stonefly. You can tie other body colors using this recipe, including green, orange, and royal blue or purple.

Hook: #14 to #18, standard wet fly or dry fly

Thread: 8/0 yellow

Body: yellow 3/0 thread or floss, double layer; red tag optional

Thorax: Hare's Ice Dubbin hare's ear blend

Hackle: partridge

Partridge and Peacock

This is a good dark caddis imitation.

Hook: #12 to #16, nymph or dry fly

Thread: 8/0 brown

Tail: scarlet red hackle fibers or marabou clump

Body: peacock herl

Ribbing: extra-small copper wire

Thorax: Hare's Ice Dubbin peacock blend

Hackle: dark partridge or grizzly

Shakey Beeley

This is one of the best attracter patterns. Tied in the larger sizes, it is particularly effective on pre-spawning browns.

Hook: #10 to #14, Tiemco TMC 2312

Thread: 6/0 coffee brown Danville

Tail: mallard flank-dyed wood duck or Hungarian partridge fibers

Body: pale yellow rabbit Zelon dubbing or tan Super Fine

Ribbing: brown Pearsall's silk thread

Collar: orange-dyed ostrich herl

Wing: Hungarian partridge with a gold or yellow Krystal Flash underwing

Starling and Red

Soft-hackle flies can be very effectively fished during a midge hatch, as the pupa is a very active swimmer. Fish these with a tiny twitch to trigger a take. You can tie other colors using this recipe, including starling and purple and starling and rust.

Hook: #20 to #24, wet fly or dry fly

Thread: 8/0 black

Body: 3/0 red thread, wound double

Hackle: starling

Yellow is a good choice for streamer color when targeting autumn brown trout. Madison River, Montana.
Photo: John Juracek

FISHING STREAMERS WITH A TENKARA ROD

When trout reach a certain size they change from eating small insects to eating large insects, like big stoneflies and grasshoppers, and leeches. Larger trout, four pounds and up—especially brown trout, lake trout, and char—want a square meal, and that means crustaceans, minnows, and even mice and lemmings. If you want to catch very large trout you should fish with streamers.

The tenkara rod can be used for fishing with flies that imitate baitfish, but only if the flies are small like some traditional wet flies or if they are unweighted, like muddler minnows. The tenkara is not so useful for casting large heavy flies. If you do get a take its difficult to set the hook because of the flexibility of the rod. Another disadvantage is that you cannot

strip in line to give action to the fly. You will have to use other means that I will describe shortly.

You will need to use small lightly weighted streamers made of soft materials like marabou feathers or rabbit fur. The current will make these flies pulse and dart like minnows. Because of the difficulty of setting the hook with tenkara, tie your flies with smaller very sharp hooks. Don't use an eight-and-a-half- or eleven-and-a-half-foot rod with streamers. Also shorten your leader to six or seven feet total length and with a 1X or 2X tippet.

A floating line will cast a heavier fly more easily than mono. Tie on a streamer using your favorite knot: clinch, nonslip loop, or turle. Cast the fly ninety degrees across the stream and mend the line downstream so the current will catch the floating line and accelerate the drift. Lead the fly with the rod and give an occasional twitch with the tip of the rod. What you are trying to do is offer a side view of an injured minnow to the fish. This is much more enticing than an end view.

Another way uses surprise to elicit a quick response. Let's say you have a large brown trout hiding under a bank on a meadow stream. Cast a large fly, like a muddler minnow, as close to the bank as possible, and slam the fly down hard and immediately pull it away with long twitches. Trout will follow the fly, and you

may have to back up to extend the retrieve. If a large, smart trout gets too long a look at a large artificial fly he usually won't take. You want to elicit an instant reaction. What do you think would happen if you suddenly surprised a predator like a grizzly bear? They love it when you run.

The technique of fishing streamer flies with a regular rod is not much different. You do have the advantage of being able to cast larger and heavier flies and use sinking lines to get down deeper where some fish hold. Also you can hand strip line in at varying speeds giving better action to the fly.

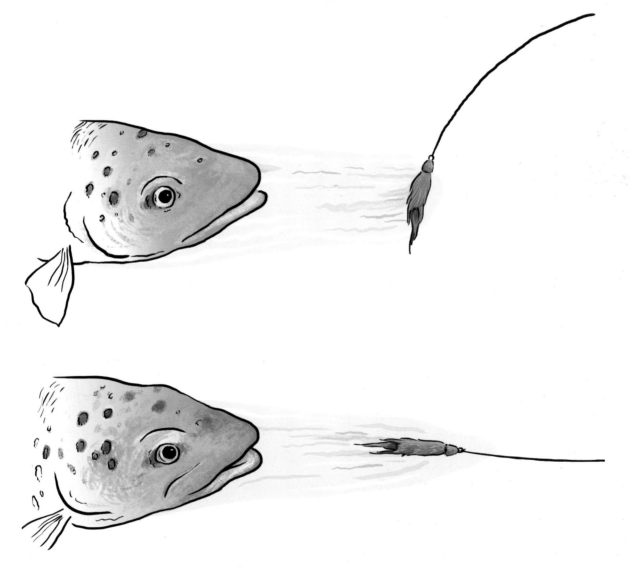

You want the fish to see the profile of your fly, not its back

RECOMMENDED STREAMERS

Rather than an exact imitation, streamers should concentrate on mobility, motion, and sometimes a little flash.

With the slow action of light trout and tenkara rods, it's difficult to get penetration in the hard mouths of large fish. It helps to use chemically sharpened hooks with small bends. Use the smallest-sized hooks in the longer lengths like 3X or 4X long. Don't go too long as the shank acts as a lever to pry the hook out.

Muddler Minnows

This imitation can be fished dry as a hopper or wet to imitate sculpins. It's even a good salmon or steelhead fly.

> Hook: #8 to #12, Gamakatsu S11-4L2H or Dai-Riki #700
>
> Thread: 3/0 black
>
> Tail: mottled turkey quill, lacquered
>
> Body: gold diamond braid
>
> Underwing: gray squirrel tail
>
> Wing: mottled turkey quill
>
> Collar: natural deer
>
> Head: natural deer

Wooly Buggers

This fly can imitate eels, minnows, and damselfly nymphs. The version below is a classic tie, but many variations are available in any fly shop.

> Hook: #8 to #12, Gamakatsu S11-4L2H
>
> Thread: 3/0 black
>
> Tail: black marabou
>
> Weight: nontoxic wire wrapped around the front third of the shank, or use a bead head
>
> Body: olive Krystal Flash chenille
>
> Hackle: black palmered

Wool-Head Sculpin

Sculpin are a favorite food for large trout. They are bottom feeders, necessitating a weighted fly. Using wool instead of spun deer hair for the collar and body helps the fly sink even faster.

Hook: #8 to #12, Gamakatsu S11-4L2H

Thread: 3/0 brown

Weight: nontoxic wire wrapped around the front third of the shank

Body: olive wool yarn

Ribbing: gold wire

Wing: a strip of light olive rabbit fur

Fins: sage grouse feathers, dyed olive

Collar and head: olive, brown, and gray clumps of wool yarn bound to the hook shank and trimmed to give a mottled effect

Soft-Hackle Streamer

This fly is simple, sinks quickly, and has lots of action. A good streamer for the tenkara rod.

Hook: #8 to #12, Gamakatsu S11-4L2H

Thread: 3/0 red, white, yellow, or black; use a thread color that contrasts with the marabou wing

Tail: two strands of silver Flashabou or pearl Krystal Flash

Wing: blood marabou wound as a hackle. The most popular colors are black, olive, yellow, white, and black/olive. The wing is followed by a turn of mallard flank feather dyed to match the marabou.

"THE KEYS TO BEING AN EFFECTIVE FLY FISHER ARE: TO KNOW WELL THE HABIT OF THE FISH, AND TO BE ABLE TO READ THE WATER."

—Mauro Mazzo

Chapter 3: Fly Fishing with Nymphs

MAURO MAZZO

When I was a kid, I spent most of my time escaping from Grandma: I would go fishing with a can of worms. Those days, I was doing everything to come home with a few fish to show my grandma. I brought home a few things that were quite borderline; when the fish don't bite, you have to go find them.

Fly fishing in Italy in the 1960s was uncommon, and to be a fly fisher was a very posh thing. Most fly fishers walked the riverbanks wearing Barbour jackets while smoking pipes. They enjoyed talking about the best fly to match the hatch, asking themselves whether it was a dun with a gray body or a yellowish-green emerger—difficult stuff for a young kid.

When I was sixteen, the father of a dear friend of mine introduced me to the world of fly fishing. I was already fishing with artificial lures, mainly for trout and pike, with good results. I was afraid that fly fishing was more of a walking and talking exercise for older people than real fishing.

I took some casting lessons. The instructor told me that only when I had acquired the right casting tempo and made the decision to fish relying only on a bunch of hair and feathers, then and only then, could I consider myself a fly fisherman—or, as they called themselves, a purist. Being a teenager, I had an interest in beautiful hair, but of another kind, and no interest at all in purity, but I decided to carry on and see what would happen on the water.

The day came to go fishing. The teacher told us to find what insects were hatching and to tie on the right imitation. Nearsighted and without polarized prescription lenses, this was a little difficult for me. I couldn't see any difference in the insects; actually, I couldn't see any hatching insects at all. So I decided to tie on a fly with a red body, just because I liked it.

Excited by the sight of rising fish, I forgot all the casting fundamentals; my fly plopped on the water, the line in loops around it. But on my second cast, I had a fish on.

A bell rang in my head. If I had a fish on after two poor casts, using a fly that I picked only because I liked the colors, fly fishing must be much easier than what the instructor told me—and also quite effective. I also realized that for nearsighted people like me, nymph fishing is the best option.

Today, after nearly forty years of fly fishing, I have not changed my mind. Fly fishing is simple and effective, and fishing with nymphs is still my favorite choice.

I have been lucky enough in my life to fish in many places around the world and for many different species of fish, from the moody Atlantic salmon to the mighty mahseer, from the elusive blue fin grayling to the ultrarare marble trout, and I believe that the keys to being an effective fly fisher are two things: to know well the habit of the fish you are trying to catch and to be able to read the water it lives in. Once you master this, even a bare hook can be the right fly.

Opposite: Mauro Mazzo fishing nymphs on the Sesia River near Quare, Italy. *Photo: Daniela Prestifilippo*

FISHING WITH NYMPHS

For years, the subsurface fishing techniques were left to the days in which nothing else was working. The majority fished a nymph without any action, like a dry fly. They didn't know what they were doing. In the last few years, however, the opposite has occurred, to the point that nymph fishing has become like rocket science. Fly fishing competitions, no matter where they are held in the world, are almost always won using nymphing techniques

When experienced anglers talk about modern nymphing techniques, they like to use exotic names like Czech, French, or Spanish nymphing. These names only serve to confuse the beginner, who wonders what the terms mean and which one is best. Don't worry; the "best technique" does not exist. What's important is to use the proper technique for the water you are fishing. Don't worry about giving your fishing technique an exotic name—a "fast blue fish from the Baltic Sea" is still just a cod.

It is interesting to note that Czech nymphing started in Poland during the 1970s on the Dunajec River by fishers who were interested in competing. Fly fishing competitions were, and still are, very popular in the countries of what was formerly called the Eastern Bloc. The people had very little means, so they had to use what was available; they were fishing with no fly lines and no reels. They used only monofilament line and very simple nymphs, and as a result always fished the nymph very close to the rod tip.

Another peculiarity of this technique was that they used heavy nymphs so the nymph would sink very fast. If you think for a second, this is quite logical. If you cast a very short line, to get the longest possible drift in the feeding zone, you want to have your flies near the bottom, where the fish are holding, in the shortest possible time. Ironically, a technique that was born to overcome a lack of means has become a fashion in our ultra-affluent society.

The evolution of nymph fishing brought more than just fancy names; it also brought some interesting developments in technique. A bunch of innovative people revisited the old, well-known techniques and, by adding a few twitches, have made nymph fishing more effective.

Akin to fishing with a worm or bait, anglers fishing nymphs today often apply action to the nymph, thereby mimicking the wiggling worm or the swimming nymph. The most important things in nymphing are getting the fly to the right depth, achieving the right speed for its drift, and giving it some action to make it look lifelike.

Theories, like the one placing importance on the exact insect imitation, faded away, switching to techniques based on the presentation of the fly at the right depth and speed. Following this new approach, you will be able to fish more or less anywhere with only a few nymphs.

When can you fish the nymph? The answer will be disappointing. Always. Nymph fishing is not limited by an event, like a hatch going on; even in the middle of a hatch, fish are still eating mostly nymphs.

Additionally, fly fishing has a casting mystique that often frightens newcomers. Casting is definitely a nice thing, but it is just one of the tools you can use to make your fishing more effective. You will soon realize that most of your fishing can be done within twenty-five feet or less.

Most of us started fishing with a pole, a piece of line, and a can of worms. No one bothered to tell us how to cast the worm, but we caught fish anyway. Why? Because we were in the right place, at the right moment, presenting to the fish what it wanted to eat.

The important thing is the ability to choose the right place, go there at the right time, and fish it in the right way. Knowledge is the key. Every piece of water has one system that works better than the others, and our aim is to teach you to figure out what is the most efficient system for that particular place and time.

The Fake Fly Box

A few years ago, Czech nymphing style was still unknown to most fishers. Sandrino, a friend of mine who competed for years with the Italian fishing team, and I booked a few days of fishing with Jiry Klima, the captain of the Czech fly fishing team. The Czech team was dominating the competition world at that time. We fished with him for several days and learned a lot. On the last day, we stopped fishing at about 6 p.m. and invited him for a beer at a bar right by the river.

Sandrino and I sat down still wearing our fishing vests, while Jiry went to the car and came back with a very nice wooden box, full of flies. "Sandrino, let's swap flies from our boxes," Jiry said as he came back in the bar. I thought it was very kind of him, but Sandrino didn't look too happy.

Jiry picked a bunch of flies from Sandrino's box and Sandrino did the same. After we had our drink and Jiry went away, I asked Sandrino why he didn't look happy about sharing the flies. He grinned, "They never give away their secret flies; I should have been prepared! The box he showed us was an ordinary fly box, whilst I showed him my competition boxes. So, he picked up some of my best flies, whilst I picked up his ordinary flies."

From that very day, I saw Sandrino swapping flies with many others. The box he pulled out was always the same one, though he had twenty more in his tackle bag.

—Mauro Mazzo

Several fly boxes of a well-known competition angler: secret flies or fakes? *Photo: Mauro Mazzo*

TENKARA NYMPHING GEAR

TENKARA NYMPHING RODS

The easiest way to learn nymph fishing is to start with a tenkara rod or with a regular outfit but without the reel. The subsurface technique that best suits a tenkara rod is short-line nymphing. The tenkara rod, because of its longer length, is one of the best rods to practice this technique. The ideal rod is ten and a half feet long: Longer rods are too affected by the action of the wind.

Considering you will often have to cast weighted flies, the most suitable action is progressive action that flexes most in the top two-thirds of its length, but not too soft. If the rod is too delicate and slow, it will be hard to set the hook.

TENKARA NYMPHING LINES AND LEADERS

Lines for nymphing are made opposite of how they should be. Heavy heads buoy downstream with the current. Nymphing lines need to be thin and light. You are not fly casting; you are lobbing. You want to get the maximum control of the fly and thus the thin, light line. For short-line nymphing, use a twelve-foot line about .025-inch diameter. It need not be tapered.

The simplest leader is made of a four- to six-foot length of 3X to 6X tippet material. Tie a perfection loop on one end and hitch it directly onto the loop at the end of the twelve-foot floating line. If you don't have a very visible color of fly line, another choice uses an eight-inch-long piece of .011-inch-thick fluorescent yellow monofilament line with a perfection loop tied at each end. This will be your bite indicator. Hitch this piece directly onto the end of your fly line and tie your leader onto the other loop with a clinch knot.

The finer the tippet, the faster the nymph will sink, and the less it will be affected by the currents. Whatever leader system you are using, only the last few inches of the fly line or indicator will be touching the water. To improve bite detection, make stripes with black waterproof marker on every inch of the fluorescent section of the tippet.

Nymphing leader with strike indicator

FISHING NYMPHS WITH A TENKARA ROD

FISHING A SINGLE NYMPH

When fishing with a single nymph, look for water with medium-slow current and a depth of two to three feet. Cast, relying only on the weight of the nymph, with a fluid arcing motion of the rod tip, forty-five degrees upstream of you. This casting technique is contrary to the traditional fly rod cast where the rod tip moves in a straight line and accelerates to an abrupt stop.

Another useful cast, especially when wading, is to let the line lay on the water behind you, and then cast it forward, using the tension of the water to load the rod. The movement is the same as an overhead cast, but without a back cast. You start with the line pulled taught by the current and cast your fly in front of you; the current dragging on your fly acts like a catapult.

Wait for a few seconds after the fly hits the water in order to let your fly get close to the bottom and then follow the nymph's path downstream with your rod tip. Try to avoid pulling the fly downstream. This is very important; the drift of the fly has to look natural. "Turbo-powered nymphs" swimming downstream faster than the current do not look natural.

But looking natural does not mean dead. If you want your fly to be effective, it has to look alive, and the best way to achieve this is to make little twitches with your rod tip during the fly's drift downstream.

These twitches have a double benefit: They imitate the movements of a nymph, and they can also trigger a reaction from the trout. In the wet fly chapter is an explanation about how to twitch your flies. I can only insist that the twitches be as small as possible. The slightest movement will be enough because the rod tip amplifies the movement. To keep direct control of the fly, keep as much line off the water as possible at all times. This is one of the most difficult things to learn because although you need to keep the line clear of the water, you do not want to pull the nymph during the drift and make it look like a hangman on a tree.

In between twitches, let your nymph drift free. I've found this combination of little twitches followed by a free drift the most attractive to fish. When the drift has reached its end and the fly starts to rise from the bottom to the surface, do not pull your fly out of the water immediately. The fish may think it is an emerging insect, and you may get a bite. Wait with the rod tip pointing downstream; sometimes the slow upward movement of the fly can persuade a doubtful trout.

You will need to develop a feel for the take. Some years ago a study was done with an expert fishing with nymphs in the old way by dead drifting the nymph on a slack line. An observer on a cliff above could see that on almost every cast a trout would take the fly and instantly spit it out without the angler even knowing.

We don't recommend large strike indicators that attach to the line. Beginners often use one to get a dead drift with a fly. We don't use them; we want direct control of the fly. You need to feel the contact and achieve a dead drift until you want to impart a subtle action when the fly is where the fish are holding. The strike indicator inhibits imparting that action and inhibits getting your fly down deep.

Fishing with nymphs you need to determine how deep the pool is. If the pool is shallow or the current is slow, use a shorter leader and a light nymph. If the pool is deep or the current is fast, choose a heavier one.

You want to stay with the lightest possible nymph that will give you a drift speed close to the current speed. As a rule of thumb, the lighter the nymph, the better the drift. The problem is the drag on the fly from the leader and the tippet. You have to use a thin tippet and the lightest possible imitation to have your fly presented to the fish in the most natural way.

Once you have hooked the fish, keep the rod tip high during the fight, using the bend of the rod to fight the fish. To land it, reach out with your hand, grab the line loosely (the line has to be free to move inside your grasp to avoid breaking in case of a sudden run by the fish), and pull the fish in gently. Whenever possible, release the fish without taking it out of the water.

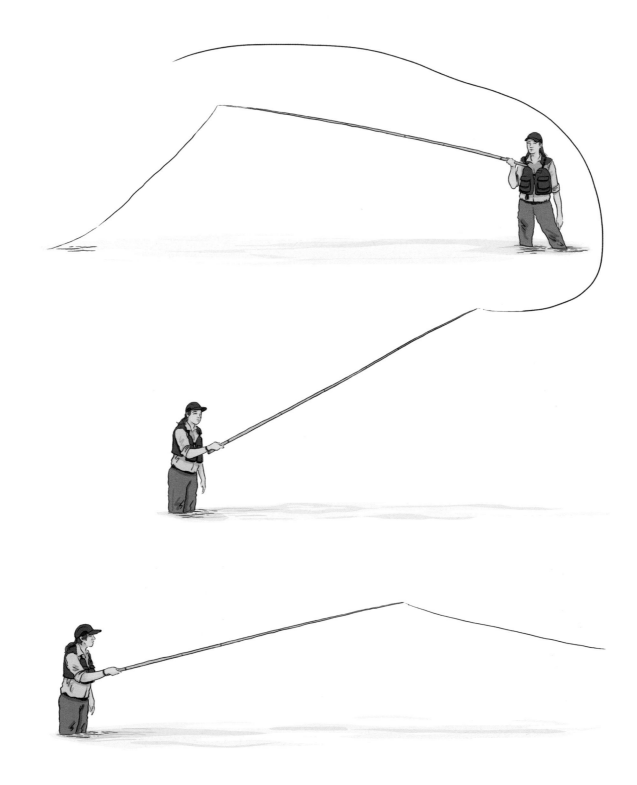

The Water Tension Cast

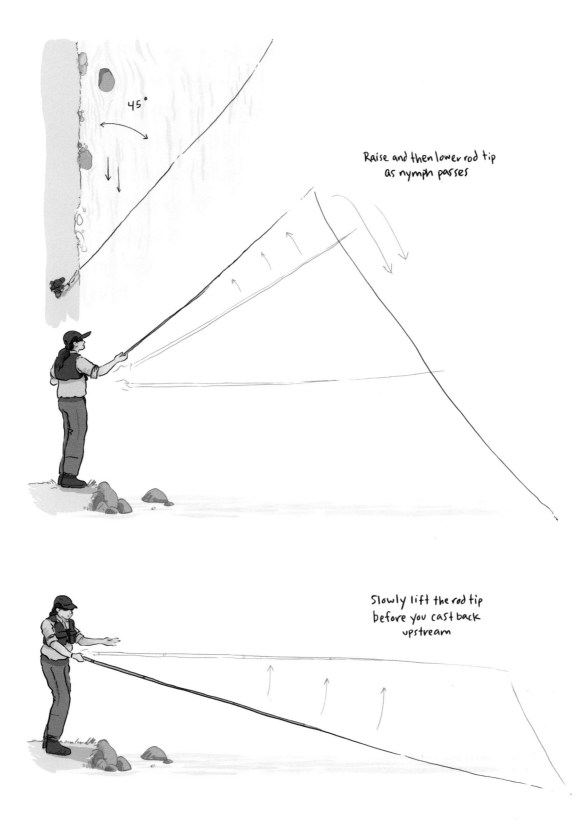

45°

Raise and then lower rod tip
as nymph passes

Slowly lift the rod tip
before you cast back
upstream

Nymph Fishing Technique

FISHING TWO OR MORE NYMPHS

Once you are familiar with fishing with one nymph, you can move on to the two-nymph rig—my favorite, particularly in medium-fast water. The two reasons for using two flies are to give the fish a choice of flies and to add more weight without having to use a larger fly. Make the tippet with the usual 3X to 5X mono, but add a six-inch dropper.

The distance between the dropper and the point fly should be about twenty to twenty-five inches; shorter in faster water, longer in slower water.

The easiest way to fish with two or more nymphs is to tie the heavier fly to the point and the lighter one to the dropper; this makes casting much easier. The most common rig is composed of a point fly, size 8 to 12 depending on the strength of the current (the stronger the current, the bigger the fly), and a dropper with a fly of size 12 to 16.

If you want to get the most natural presentation in slow current or with difficult fish, you can tie the smallest fly to the point. This will make the presentation more natural, but casting and bite detection will be much more difficult. For this reason, I suggest this rig only to people with a lot of experience. A good alternative for less experienced people is to use two small flies (14 or 16) of the same weight for both point and dropper.

The presentation is the same when fishing with two or more flies as when fishing with one. Because two or more flies are often used in fast current, you only need to change the angle at which you cast the fly to get the longest possible drift. The faster the current, the more upstream you will need to make your cast—up to ninety degrees in very fast currents. This is necessary to get a long enough drift for your flies.

You will have to make the action more dynamic. And you will have to lift the rod tip in the first half following the drift and lower it in the second half. The take will often be very hard, so detecting the bite in this kind of water is not that difficult.

HOW THE TWO-FLY NYMPH RIGS WORK

- Flies with same weight: The tippet drifts parallel to the bottom. This rig is good for exploring more water in the same drift at the same depth.

- Heavier point fly: The tippet drifts in a more vertical orientation. This helps when you want to explore two different levels of the water column.

- Heavier dropper fly: The point fly, in spite of its light weight, will run close to the bottom with a very natural drift.

Mauro Mauzo tight-line nymphing for marble trout. Sesia River, Italy. *Photo: Daniela Prestifilippo*

NYMPH FISHING WITH ROD AND REEL

Fishing with the rod only will oblige you to be very efficient with your fishing action. You can compare this to taking a picture with a manual camera with a fixed lens versus using an automatic camera with a zoom lens.

With a simple manual camera, you have only the aperture and focus to play with. Using a modern auto SLR camera with zoom gives you thousands of options, but unless you are a pro, you will not be able to fully utilize these options. You will take the occasional nice shot, but more often than not, it will be only by chance.

To master a craft, you have to achieve total control of the tool you are using. Photographers like Henri Cartier-Bresson, Robert Capa, and Elliott Erwitt made their masterpieces using only fixed lenses and manual cameras. Fishing is the same: Learning with a very simple tool, with very few options available, will teach you how to get the best out of your tackle.

Once you have learned to fish without a reel, the transition to regular rod and reel will be quite easy. You will know from your tenkara experience that to catch fish you do not need to cast a mile. The ability to cast farther will be only an extra tool, not the foundation of your fishing.

If you are not a strong caster yet and are using a light nymph, you may want to add a butt section to your setup. Tie a loop in both ends of a three-foot length of .013-inch monofilament line, and hitch one end to the end of your fly line. To this hitch your fluorescent bite indicator with your leader tied to the other end.

The ideal rod is a nine- to ten-foot progressive action one, meaning that the rod bends all through its length but gets stiffer toward the butt. The shorter option allows more precise casting; the longer one gives you better control of the nymphs during their drift.

The most important thing with the rod and reel is the balance of the rod. With most nymph fishing techniques, you have to fish for hours with your arm lifted to keep as much line as possible off the water. A well-balanced, light rod and reel will make your life a lot easier and will avoid that heavy tip feeling that makes you tire quickly. Use a large arbor reel, as it reduces the coiling of the fly line.

When fishing with nymphs, most often you will be casting weighted flies, so the lightest line you can handle is the best choice. When casting weighted flies, the weight of the fly helps you reach the distance you want (comparable to spin fishing), even though you are using a light rod and line. Conventional wisdom says you have to use a heavy line to cast heavy flies; you are supposed to load the rod with the weight of the line only. But this approach would oblige you to use very heavy lines, seven weight or more, and that would make it impossible to fish with the techniques described here.

I want to make it clear that to a nymph fisher, the only real advantage of a fly line and a reel is the ability to change the length of the line out of the tip and the ability to control that line. You can do short- or long-line nymphing. Apart from this, when nymph fishing, you will be better off using a monofilament line. The monofilament, thanks to its thin diameter, which is less than half of the thinnest fly line, is less subject to the action of the wind, which allows you to detect subtle takes. It is also less exposed to the action of the current, which facilitates a natural drift for your nymph. You don't need a separate spool for your reel loaded with monofilament. Just loop a forty-foot section of monofilament shooting line onto the tip of your fly line.

When fishing with a light downstream wind, you can take the advantage of the fact that the monofilament is half the diameter of the thinnest fly line, and you just keep your rod close to the water. When the wind is strong, if you keep the rod high you will make a big bow in your line that will drag your fly faster than the current. To defeat this drag, as soon as your fly hits the water, mend upstream and lay the line down on the water. Follow the drift with the tip of the rod, mending if necessary, and when the indicator stops strike sideways and upstream.

The bare truth is that you don't really need a fly line, but to make casting easier when fishing very light nymphs, get the lightest line possible. For all-purpose nymphing, the ideal rod is a four weight, set up with a one- or two-weight line.

You need to adjust your casting to this peculiar rig. Reduce false casting to a minimum, because when

One of the world's greatest freestone rivers: The Madison, with its boulders and pockets, is ideal water for nymphing.
Photo: John Juracek

using weighted flies, the only thing false casting does is increase the chances of tangling the leader.

As soon as the fly touches the water, you have to try to maintain contact with the flies. This is very important because the fish might take the fly during its descending path and you have to be ready to strike immediately. A good way to maintain contact with the flies is to keep the fly line under your index finger during the cast. When the fly hits the water, stop the line by pushing your finger against the rod handle and start retrieving the line using the other hand to take up the slack.

When following the drift of the flies, try to keep the rod tip close to the water and shorten the line using the left hand (when holding the rod with the right hand).

With rod and reel, you can make longer casts, but don't forget that this does not mean you are obliged to do so. The best fishing is often close to the bank, and being cautious and silent when approaching the bank will help you be successful.

A big advantage you get from the reel comes when fighting a big fish. The reel offers you the possibility to play the fish with ease, letting line out and retrieving it in accordance with the behavior of the fish. Please bear in mind that playing a fish for too long can overstress the fish.

The Usual Question

I was fishing the Firehole River in Yellowstone Park while a big hatch was going on, and I was doing really well with two small nymphs, which I was fishing just under the surface.

I watched a young boy running up and down the river casting a big dry fly here and there, followed by his mother carrying a large landing net. I could tell he had no idea what he was doing.

He came by and asked me the usual question, "What fly are you using?" His mother explained that he was supposed to be hiking with his group, but all he wanted to do was fish.

I changed his rig, tying on a very simple leader, made of seven feet of mono, and tied on a nymph under a piece of yarn to be used as a strike indicator.

His casting was very basic, so I told him to cast very close to the bank, behind a rock that was hiding him from the fish. After a few casts, he had his first fish on. His eyes were sparkling, and I knew he was caught on fly fishing.

—Mauro Mazzo

The Firehole River, Yellowstone National Park, Wyoming. *Photo: John Juracek*

TYING NYMPHS

My nymphs are tied very simply. These patterns are mainly searching nymphs, but they catch fish, showing once more that the exact imitation theory is not always right. The priority is to offer a fly similar to what the fish are eating at the right depth and drift. The weight of the fly, and its disposition, has a very important role; the dressing itself is more impressionistic than realistic.

There are ultrarealistic imitations in the nymph world, but I have never seen anyone catch many fish with them. Their place is really in a nice cabinet in your house rather than on the riverbank.

I believe that names are good with insects and dry or wet flies, but with most nymphs, apart from the famous ones, names are rather confusing. Maybe anglers don't feel it's very cool to tell people they fish only Pheasant Tails or Hare's Ears, so they give their flies exotic names like PT Cruiser, or Tollett's™ Half-Juiced. So rather than suggesting fly X or Y, I will try to give some basic information that will allow you to fish in most waters.

For a dark stream bottom, use a dark fly; for a light stream bottom, use a light fly. For faster or deeper water, use a big fly tied on a size 8 to 12 hook, and weight it heavily with tungsten bead heads and/ or nontoxic wire. For slower or shallower water, use a small fly tied on a size 12 to 16 hook and weighted only with a bead head or only with wire. For the smallest sizes (16 to 20), use only 2X strong nymph hooks with no weight. As you can see, it is not rocket science.

Bear in mind that with only ten imitations, tied on different-sized hooks, you can embark on a world fly fishing tour. With the nymphs I describe in the following pages, I have caught fish all over the world, from trout to steelhead, from Atlantic salmon to grayling. I believe they are all you need to cover 90 percent of situations.

SOME TIPS

The tips that follow are valid for all nymphs and will help you decide which flies to choose for your box.

- Use bent, or jig, hooks, weighted in the top or middle of the shank to reduce the chance of snagging flies on the bottom. This kind of fly is preferred when fishing rivers with an uneven bottom or one full of debris.

- A thin body makes the fly sink faster; a coarse, fluffy body slows down the sink rate of the fly. So a thin body is preferred in fast water; a fluffy body in slower water.

- Silver or gold bead heads work better in colored water. Brass, black, or no bead heads are good for clear water.

Cased Caddis Imitation

Hook: #10 and #12, jig, 2X long, 2X wire

Bead head: gold or black, 3 mm

Tail: green or yellow fluorescent wool or floss

Body: Hare's dubbing with a color that matches natural insects

Legs: a couple of turns of partridge hackle

Uni Nymph – light

Hook: #12 and #14

Bead head: gold, 2 to 3 mm

Tail: partridge hackle fiber

Body: beige Hare's dubbing

Thorax: Hare's Ice Dubbin peacock blend

Rib: copper wire

Collar: orange floss (Optional turn of partridge hackle before the floss adds a lifelike effect.)

Uni Caddis Larvae - light

Hook: #12 to #16, grub

Body: beige dubbing

Thorax: dark brown and orange dubbing

Back: elastic vinyl, with five or six turns of nylon monofilament around the body keeping the back in place, imitates a scud

Uni Nymph – green

Hook: #14 and #16, grub

Bead head: gold, 2.5 mm

Tail: furnace rooster hackle fiber

Body: bluish-green Hare's dubbing

Collar : fluorescent orange floss

Uni Emerger Nymph - light

    Hook: #16 and #18

    Bead head: gold, 2 mm

    Tail: grey hen or rooster hackle fiber

    Body: light grey or beige Hare's dubbing

    Thorax: peacock herl

    Collar: hen grey hackle

Hare's Ear

    Hook: #12 to #16, 2X long, 2X heavy

    Tail: partridge

    Ribbing: copper wire

    Body: various shades of hare's ear

    Thorax: Hare's Ice Dubbin grey

    Wing case: goose quill or magic shrimp foil

    Hackle: partridge

    Colored collar: optional

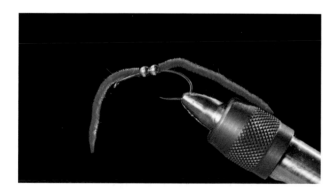

San Juan Worm

    Hook: #8 to #12, grub, 2X long, 2X gape

    Bead head: gold, 3 to 4 mm

    Body: red or pink chenille

Uni Caddis Larvae - dark

Hook: #8 to #12, grub

Body: dark brown or dark green dubbing with red spot

Thorax: peacock herl

Back: elastic vinyl, kept in place with five or six turns of dark nylon monofilament, or copper wire around the body

Uni Stonefly Nymph

Hook: #8 to #10, grub, 2X long, 2X gape

Bead head: orange, 4 to 5 mm

Tail: pheasant tail fibers

Body: pheasant tail fibers

Thorax: Hare's Ear Ice Dubbin peacock blend

Rib: copper wire

Uni Mayfly Nymph

Hook: #10 to #14, 2X long, 2X gape

Bead head: gold, 2.5 to 4 mm

Tail: pheasant tail fibers

Body: pheasant tail fibers

Thorax: Hare's Ear Ice Dubbin peacock blend

Rib: copper wire

Legs: partridge hackle on top with V shape

Back: dark pheasant tail fibers

Collar: orange floss

Uni Nymph Jig Hook

Hook: #12 to #16, jig, 2X long, 2X gape

Bead head: gold, 2 to 2.5 mm

Tail: pheasant tail fibers

Body: dark brown Hare's dubbing

Thorax: white Hare's dubbing

Collar: orange floss

Uni Emerger Nymph - dark

    Hook: #14 to #18, grub, 2X length, 2X gape

    Bead head: gold, 2 to 2.5 mm

    Tail: furnace hackle

    Body: in greenish-brown Hare's dubbing

    Collar: one turn of grey hen hackle

Sawyers Pheasant Tail Nymph

    Hook: #12 to #16, 2X long, 2X gape

    Tail: pheasant tail fibers

    Body: pheasant tail fibers

    Thorax: copper wire

    Rib: copper wire

    Wing case: pheasant tail fibers

NYMPHING FOR ANADROMOUS FISH

There are times when nymphing techniques are the most effective way to fish for steelhead, Atlantic salmon, and sea trout.

- When the water is cold in the morning or in the winter when the fish won't move very far to chase a swinging fly.

- When steelhead are near spawning pink or sockeye salmon, they want to eat those eggs!

- When the water is warm in the dog days of summer and the salmon have gone dour.

- Whenever anadromous fish (for whatever reason) are schooled up in deep pools.

- When in Southeast Alaska and spring steelhead are often reluctant to take swinging flies and really prefer egg patterns.

- When fishing for hatchery fish who hardly know what an insect is. They want a fish pellet or smelly egg.

All anadromous fish are suckers for worms and gobs of cured smelly salmon eggs. In Iceland after the season closes, and the catch-and-release sports have left, the farmers go out with their cans of worms and catch their winter supply of salmon.

If you can see fish holed up in a deep pool, there is a good chance you can catch them—and sometimes every one of them. These big fish in deep water feel secure and are not spooked by lines, heavy leaders, or even humans standing ten feet away. The method is simple: drift a rubber-legged stonefly nymph pattern past their noses, and give a little twitch. The important thing is to get the fly down to their level so all they have to do is open their mouths and suck it in.

All fishers have their weaknesses; that's why we have a reputation for lying. There are times when no matter how skillful we are, we go through long periods when we can't catch a fish. Atlantic salmon, with all their neuroses, especially can drive you to drink. Steelhead are easy; they will take almost any fly, but there are so few of them left. In our desperation, we hear the siren songs of the scented egg or the heavily weighted Snelda or Red Francis, and we look jealously at the spin fisher tossing his sacks of Gooey Bob eggs and hoovering up fish after fish. You can avoid the temptation of the sirens with cotton plugs in your ears . . . or just pull out those nymphs.

It is an effective method, but it might not be everyone's cup of tea. It might be an alternative for those days on which endlessly swinging a fly is like watching the same movie five times and expecting a different ending.

Sonya Pask with a perfect Skeena River steelhead. *Photo: Tim Pask*

A Tenkara Salmon

When Atlantic salmon first move into a river on their spawning run, they seem to be in a terrible hurry to get somewhere. They jump as they enter a pool and, seconds later, jump again as they leave it. It can be frustrating times for the angler, because the fish are not much interested in stopping to take a fly. Not until a day or two later when they settle down into a comfortable lie and out of habit, boredom, or to defend their spot, they may fall for a bunch of feathers on a hook.

Fishing in the Haffjardara River in Iceland recently we were blessed with a good run of grilse and small salmon. At the riffle area of the upper Aquarium pool, as a lark I decided to see if I could manage a salmon on soft-hackle flies and my twenty-five-year-old tenkara rod.

I put an eight-foot extender onto my twenty-foot floating line as I wanted to keep farther away from these spooky fish. I tied a Shakey Beeley onto the 2X tippet and a blue and partridge soft hackle with a red tag onto the dropper—both tied on size 12, up-turned-eye light salmon hooks. On my second cast, right after I gave the fly a twitch, a five-pound grilse took the dropper. Surprisingly, it wasn't as difficult to land as an equivalent rainbow or brown trout, which after feeling the hook, tend to streak away immediately. I landed four more that day and lost twice as many for various reasons. One I lost was a large salmon that broke off in the Count pool when I panicked and failed to throw the rod for fear of losing it in the rapids below.

Later during the week, I landed a dozen more with a few in the seven-pound-plus proper salmon range. Three times I had to throw the rod in the river when I couldn't stop the fish on its initial run. To tell the truth, the first time it happened, the rod was actually ripped out of my hand. I ran as fast as I could in the waist deep water but never could catch up to my waking rod handle. But after seventy-five yards, I saw my rod turn and come back upstream. I ran back up and caught up with it near where the fish first took the fly. Later, I started to notice a pattern in the fight. After the pressure is off, the salmon (like a large trout) wants to return to its secure lie. Its querencia. However, I don't recommend you try this craziness unless you have a good run out—the inevitable rodeo needs plenty of room.

—Yvon Chouinard

Photo: Malinda Chouinard
Opposite: Let's rodeo! Yvon Chouinard fishing for grilse in Iceland. *Photo: Malinda Chouinard*

Chapter 4: Fly Fishing with Dry Flies

CRAIG MATHEWS

When I was four years old, my parents started taking my brother, Tom, and me to Silver Lake near our home in Grand Rapids. We spent the summers there, and I learned to fish for bluegill and bass. Every evening, we'd watch three fly fishermen wade out into the lake and cast their bamboo fly rods. It was magic to see their fly lines cutting the evening air, and they would hook up often and bring to net big bluegill, crappie, or bass.

One night, I mustered the gumption to join in their fly fishing lineup. I took my grandfather's bamboo rod hooked above the wooden frame of our walkout basement door, opened the door, walked out, and promptly closed the screen door on the rod, busting about a foot off the end. Undaunted, I waded into the lake toward the anglers. One of the men, who lived in a log cabin nearby, motioned me over and gave me a short casting lesson along with a couple of small poppers and a rubber Spider Fly. It was only a few casts before I was into a four-inch bluegill. I took a few more that first evening and was hooked on fly fishing for life.

A few days later, we were driving home from grocery shopping and saw the same three men walking from a bridge into the woods not far from our summer place. My mom dropped Tom and me off and waited in the car for us. We snuck up on the men and found them rigging up their tackle at a pond in the forest. I'll never forget the fish rising to the surface of the pond that day. Not knowing what they were, we sat watching, and then approached when one of the men landed one—a brook trout with brilliant spots on its flanks. I was hooked again and began learning all I could about fly fishing for trout.

Later, after I graduated from college, Larry Dech and I headed west to fish Yellowstone country and its incredible fly fishing opportunities. Not long after, my wife, Jackie, and I came to Yellowstone in September to fish for two weeks. We returned home, and a month later, we schemed to move to Yellowstone, which we did later that winter. I came as the police chief of West Yellowstone, and she was a police dispatcher.

A few years later, we opened Blue Ribbon Flies and began fly tying and fishing for a living. We fish over one hundred days a year and talk about it daily with our friends and customers.

Over the years, I went from fishing dry flies exclusively to solely fishing nymphs, then to streamers, and back to fishing dry flies again. There is nothing I enjoy more than watching a trout come up for a dry fly. I now fish dries over 80 percent of my time on the water, and I use a tenkara rod over 50 percent of the time. I enjoy its effectiveness, efficiency, and simplicity.

Most fly fishers feel there is magic on our planet, and it is held in our rivers, lakes, and streams. Henry David Thoreau once said, "Many men go fishing all their lives without knowing that it is not fish they are after." Most of us sooner or later discover that fly fishing helps preserve our capacity for wonder. Pursuing wild fish with a fly rod can teach us to see, smell, and feel the miracles of stream life with the serenity and the beauty of nature all around.

Opposite: Craig Mathews on O'Dell Creek with a nice brown that took a terrestrial imitation. Montana. *Photo: Mauro Mazzo*

FISHING WITH DRY FLIES

Evening mayfly hatch on the Madison River. During these May/June (early season) hatches there are fish in many of the pockets created by rocks.   *Photo: Jake Hawkes*

My favorite method of fly fishing is with the dry fly. I enjoy the visual aspect of it. I prefer the stalk and the hunt: I enjoy slowly patrolling the banks of rivers, ponds, and streams searching for the telltale ring of a rise, a trout's back or snout breaking the surface as the fish rises to a mayfly, caddis, or midge. To me, there is nothing more satisfying than getting as close to the rising trout as possible, whether slowly sliding along the bank on my butt or wade-walking in the river on my knees.

If I do not find fish actively rising to insect activity when I arrive on a stream, I can usually find one or two coming to the surface if I am patient and "sit on water." By this I mean I locate a quiet pool, pocket, or slow run where trout hold and feel secure. I find a comfortable spot along the shore and sit, watching the surface for a telltale ring of a subtle rise or a fish's

tail or dorsal fin barely breaking the surface. Then I go back to my old profession as a police detective to find the clues of what the river is telling me to do. Are there midges emerging or mayflies? Are there ants on the water? When I discover what is bringing the trout to feed on the surface, I knot on an imitation and begin my fishing day.

If I do not see a rise, I might tie on an attractor pattern, a fly that imitates nothing in particular but may entice a rise. I prospect with my attractor pattern, covering much more water than I normally would with rising trout. Often, the attractor fly moves a fish to come up and take a look at it without taking it. I then tie on a pattern that imitates an insect the fish are used to seeing—an ant, beetle, or mayfly I know could be active at that time—and present it.

My First Time with a Tenkara Rod

The first time I saw a tenkara rod was a few years ago on O'Dell Spring Creek near my home in the Madison Valley of Montana. Yvon had come to spend a few days fishing with me. We arrived at the creek, and Yvon stowed the rod in the rear pocket of his vest, explaining that he and Mauro had fished the rod recently on a small stream in Wyoming and had had a fun day fooling cutthroat trout. I couldn't help smiling to myself as I followed behind thinking about hooking and landing a huge spring creek brown trout on the delicate tenkara rod with a fixed-length line and no reel.

We both fished our traditional rod-and-reel setups that morning. After lunch, Yvon finally pulled out his tenkara rod and tied on a small Blue-Winged Olive soft hackle and proceeded to catch several nice browns up to fifteen inches.

I marveled at how efficient Yvon could be using short casts, swinging his soft-hackle flies in all the likely looking spots—undercut pockets and pools—where trout jumped all over his presentations.

When he offered to let me try the rod, I quickly knotted on a grasshopper fly and cast it upstream a short distance to the next undercut bank. A fourteen-inch rainbow gobbled the hopper, I set, and both trout and I were hooked on tenkara.

—Craig Mathews

Choosing the right fly on O'Dell Spring Creek, Montana. *Photo: Mauro Mazzo*

Seeing the Light

Last December, a couple moved to town and stopped by the shop complaining about having to wait several months before they could fish dry flies. I told them to get a fishing license immediately and a couple of midge dry flies and head down to the Madison River to fish trout rising to midges. They made their purchase, and I drew them a map of where to find surface-feeding trout.

A week later, they stopped back in and when questioned admitted they'd been on the river three days and had yet to see a fish rise but did have some great nymph fishing. Our winter guide, Dan, was tying flies that morning, and I asked him to take the couple to the river and show them some rising trout. The couple drifted back in later that same day and sheepishly told me Dan "showed us the light!"

They told me they walked to the river and stood while Dan sat on the bank and asked, "Do you see the rising trout?" Both thought Dan was kidding them until they too sat down and watched. Simply sitting on the bank put their eyes on a level with the surface of the river: The subtle rises to tiny midges became evident. Dan told me later, "You should have seen their eyes bug out when they saw all the fish coming to the surface."

—Craig Mathews

A rainbow trout rises to a mayfly. *Photo: Barry and Cathy Beck*

TENKARA DRY FLY GEAR

TENKARA DRY FLY RODS

You don't need to invest $1,000 in a rod, reel, and line to start fishing tenkara. Most tenkara rods sell for $150 to $250. I prefer Temple Fork Outfitter's eleven-and-a-half-foot soft-action carbon fiber tenkara rod for most of my dry fly fishing. The rod bends uniformly throughout, from butt to tip. I can easily load the rod and feel the loading of the line to allow a perfect forward cast without a tailing loop causing a tangle. This slow-action rod protects fine tippets and casts well into the wind. TFO's eight-and-a-half-foot rod works best for small streams and those waters with brushy banks and overhangs.

TENKARA DRY FLY LINES AND LEADERS

Effective dry fly fishing with tenkara rods requires the use of one of two lines available to anglers on the market today. I prefer either a traditional furled or a fine-diameter level floating fly line. A furled line is one fashioned from several twisted, small-diameter fly-tying threads. Both work fine, but the furled line requires some babysitting, as you need to apply fly or line floatant to it from time to time to keep it floating on the surface.

Furled lines are very soft and supple and transmit the energy of the cast easily, making for efficient line and tippet turnover and great fly presentation. Furled lines come in various lengths. I prefer the thirteen-foot length. They easily attach to the rod end as they come with a hitching loop that you can hitch onto the braided lillian at the end of the rod. These also come with a stainless steel ring on the leader end to which I add appropriate leader and tippets from 4X to 7X.

The other option, traditional level fly lines, are inexpensive and can be purchased complete in 80- to 100-foot lengths or bought in lengths cut from spools at most fly shops. I prefer a level line .021 inches in diameter, eight to fifteen feet long. Or better yet, cut both ends out of a DT000 line: one eight feet and the other fifteen feet in length. Both lines require tying a turle knot to loop over the lillian (see drawing on page 35). Leave a one-inch tag in the turle knot to loosen it in order to remove it from the lillian when not fishing. On my leader end of the line, I usually nail knot (see drawing on page 94) a standard seven-and-a-half-foot leader tapered to 3X or 4X and add tippets as needed.

KNOTS

Most anglers spend more time learning knots than they do learning to read the water or the insects that bring the trout to the surface. While knots are important to anglers, there are only a few that fly fishers must know. One secures the fly and the other ties on the tippet. A clinch or improved clinch knot is the easiest and best to learn for tying on the dry fly. The strongest for tippet-leader connections is the double-surgeon's knot (see page 39).

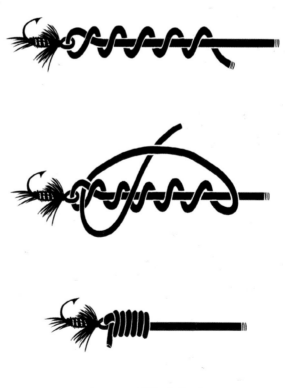

Improved Clinch Knot

DRY FLY FISHING WITH A TENKARA ROD

As a rule, if you see fish rising, approach from downstream and work directly upstream. It is always best not to wade and to stay low to the bank so as not to present a silhouette that will spook the trout. If you must wade, by approaching from downstream you will not send debris and wading waves to the fish and signal your approach. Try to get within fifteen feet of the rising fish. Then present your fly about two feet upstream of the rising fish using a fixed-length, short-line, pinpoint-accurate cast (described below).

Allow the fly to approach the rising fish, and as the line begins to float back toward you, raise the rod by gradually bringing it up from a nine o'clock position to a twelve o'clock position, taking up the slack line as the line returns in the current. This allows the fly to float naturally and not be dragged by the downstream tension on the line from the current. It also keeps you in touch with your fly so when the fish does take the fly, you can set the hook and drive it home without having to take in slack line. If the fish does

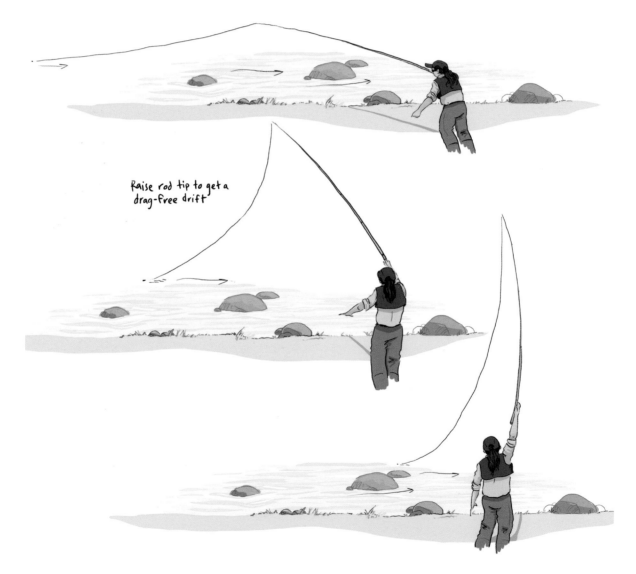

Raise rod tip to get a drag-free drift

Upstream Dry Fly Fishing Technique

90

not take your offering, allow the fly to pass a foot or two beyond it and recast.

If searching water and fishing when no fish are rising, present your flies to all likely looking areas you expect trout to hold in with the same presentation as above. Wade slowly and carefully upstream prospecting the water as you go.

There are times when a fish rises upstream or downstream of your position or near an obstruction like a weed bed, boulder, or mixed currents and prevents an upstream approach. In those cases, carefully wade from above or below to the rising fish. If wading from upstream, be careful not to send a wading wave or debris and spook the fish. Get as close to the fish as you can, preferably within twenty feet, and cast downstream, or upstream and across, with a slack-line accurate presentation. If wading downstream to the fish, mend once or twice as the fly drifts to the rising trout to delay drag and avoid a skittering/waking fly. The aim is to present the fly as naturally as possible.

I prefer the upstream approach, but nothing is set in stone. Do whatever it takes to get close to a rising fish. Line drag is your enemy, and getting close to a rising fish helps to delay drag and stay in touch with your fly.

Check cast

Lower rod tip to get a drag-free drift

Downstream Dry Fly Fishing Technique

How to Make a Short, Slack, Pinpoint-Accurate Cast

The reason for using this cast is to delay drag on the fly. There are several ways to accomplish this cast, but my favorites are listed below. The two methods work with both tenkara and standard fly fishing gear.

With the first method, I choose the target, and if fishing standard rod and reel, I carry a bit of extra line in my line hand. If fishing tenkara, I let a short amount of slack line hang from the end of the rod. With tenkara, I never present a full-length line-and-leader cast that lands on a tight line, as this would usually result in immediate drag.

I guesstimate the spot I want my fly to land while accounting for current speed and drag. On my forward stroke, I aim for the spot where I want the fly to land. With tenkara, I make sure the extra line

I cast allows enough slack to land on the water and give the fly time to drift naturally to the targeted fish. If fishing standard rod and reel and carrying extra line in my line hand, I stop the rod tip near the end of my forward stroke and at the same time release the extra slack line from my line hand, which allows the fly to reach my target with enough slack line to delay drag. This method will come naturally with a little experience.

With the second method, I follow the same two steps as with the first. On the third step, I aim for the spot; however, this time I follow through on the forward stroke and allow the fly to shoot beyond the target. As the line straightens, I stop my rod tip, causing the line to recoil and create slack line in a series of S-curves on the water. This method requires a feel and developed intuition, but with experience, it will become second nature.

ADVANCED TENKARA DRY FLY TECHNIQUES

I usually fish one dry fly, but at times I knot on a second trailing dropper fly. Usually this occurs when I cannot determine what the fish are feeding on. During mayfly, caddis, or midge hatches, I might come upon several rising fish, and to quickly determine what stage of the insect the trout are feeding on, I tie on an emerger and a dun for instance.

To do this, leave a six- to eight-inch tag from your leader-tippet connection knot and tie one fly on here and the other on the end of your tippet. The distance between the leader-tippet connection knot to the point fly is eighteen to twenty-four inches.

Make sure the tag end is the heavier of the two pieces as this helps keep the mono from tangling. Present the two flies, and whatever pattern works best, remove the other fly and go with a one-fly presentation from there. Fishing two dry flies at the same time usually results in more tangles and hooks in the net mesh or your fingers when trying to release fish, but it is worth it when you are trying to find out what the fish are feeding on.

Another time when I may use two flies and wade from an upstream position is during caddis emergences or egg-laying periods as fish take flies skittered on the surface or hovering just above the surface of the river. Then, I knot a dry caddis pattern on the tag end of my leader-tippet section and trail a weighted caddis pupa. The idea is the weighted fly on the point breaks the surface tension of the water and allows the trailing dry fly to skitter on, or above, the surface. It is fun to watch big trout jump out of the water to take your dry fly offering. This is the one time I want drag to occur to keep my dry fly dancing on, or above, the surface of the river.

The Gift

This last summer, I fished with my tenkara rod on the Firehole River in Yellowstone Park. I arrived as caddisflies were hatching and trout rose to them in the riffles and pools. I tied on an Iris Caddis emerger pattern and began taking a trout on almost every cast; with the tenkara, I could skip and dance my fly in each area where the trout were rising.

I heard a noise along the bank and turned to find several spectators lined up along the shore behind me. One young boy was at my hip, his mother apologizing, saying, "I'm sorry he got so close to you; he'd love to learn to fly-fish." I replied, "Well, we'll take care of that right now." We walked a short distance to the next riffle with half the audience in tow. Within a few minutes, the lad had landed eight rainbows. I gave him the rod and he was on his way.

—Craig Mathews

Matteo releases a nice marble trout hybrid. At twelve years old, his motto is "a bad day of fishing is better than a good day at school." *Photo: Mauro Mazzo*

DRY FLY FISHING WITH A ROD AND REEL

DRY FLY RODS

For rod-and-reel dry fly fishing, I like a slow, even-action rod. A slow rod forces me to slow down between casts and load the rod properly to recast, and to concentrate on my fly, the rises of fish, and the insects fish are feeding on. You need to get close to rising trout, and the slow action allows you to load the rod quickly with a short line and recast quickly too.

Slow-action rods also protect the fine tippets required in dry fly fishing by absorbing the shock of the trout taking the fly. My favorite traditional dry fly rod, while slow action, still has enough backbone to allow me to defeat heavy winds, pick line off the water, and present large bushy flies without false casting.

I like a simple single-action fly reel that is lightweight and has a click drag. There are many fine reels available that provide a good drag system and hold fifty yards of backing and can handle big, wild trout in heavy currents.

DRY FLY LINES, LEADERS, AND TIPPETS

The fly line is one of the foundations of successful dry fly fishing, yet few know much about them. Today's lines are made to last many days of use on rivers, lakes, and streams without babysitting. They need no maintenance except keeping them clean; they will float well and give many days of use.

Most weight-forward lines take up to 30 percent less space on reels than do double-tapered lines. And the same weight double-tapered and weight-forward lines have the same basic taper for the first thirty feet. Since nearly all my dry fly casting is done within thirty feet, I prefer the weight-forward line. With it I can put plenty of backing on my reel and make all my casts and presentations.

Even though there are hundreds of choices of leaders, it really is not that complicated. For dry fly fishing, I begin with a nine-foot knotless leader tapered down to 4X tippet.

Tie a three- to four-turn nail knot to connect the leader to the fly line using a simple nail knot tool. Add appropriate tippets of 5X, 6X, or 7X to the end of the leader depending on the fishing at hand.

If fishing a big salmonfly or grasshopper dry fly, cut the leader back a foot to 3X and knot the fly on there.

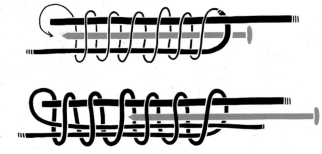

Nail Knot

Kenkara

Tenkara is also a useful tool for the seasoned angler. Ken lives along the White and Norfolk Rivers in Arkansas, where trout are often measured in pounds rather than inches. On his first visit to our shop in Yellowstone last summer, I showed him a tenkara rod. He laughed and said something like, "What fish could you catch with that little stick?" Ken stopped by our fly shop daily, and over the next several days I caught him discreetly listening to the ongoing discussions on the merits of tenkara techniques. Finally, one day, acting a bit agitated at our tenkara tales, Ken said, "OK, I'll bite, just give me one of those dang things, and I'll bet I break it on a Madison River brown trout today." Two hours later, Ken ran into the store babbling a story about catching his first nineteen-inch brown trout and several rainbows on his new rod. Today, his email address begins with "Kenkara."

—Craig Mathews

Spring weather is often hit or miss. Madison River, Montana. *Photo: Jay Beyer*

SKILLS AND GUIDELINES FOR DRY FLY FISHING

Both expert and beginning fly fishers usually feel the most important ingredient to successful fly fishing is the right fly pattern. Yet the two most important things anglers—tenkara or rod and reel—must learn to be successful are proper presentation and technique. Too many anglers put their faith in realistic flies and long casts. And while some might agree proper presentation is the foundation of effective fly fishing, few actually practice the basics.

One day on a favorite spring creek where big trout are hard to approach and catch, I watched an old man creep along at a snail's pace, never wading but using streamside cover to get within fifteen to twenty feet of rising trout. He used a short, soft, pinpoint, slack-line cast to defeat drag and took several big fish. That same day, I watched another angler who advocates powerful rods and long presentations bang out sixty-to eighty-foot casts and spook every trout he fished to. He failed to take even one trout that day.

Here are a few tips on approaching the river during a hatch or covering water when there are no insects bringing fish to the surface.

- If you want to fish dry flies during an insect emergence, be on the water when they are expected. Check weather forecasts as well as wind and water conditions.

- Observe other anglers, if present, to see what direction they are heading to avoid crowding.

- Observe the conditions. Is there insect activity like caddis or mayfly, terrestrials or midges? If there are no insects or rises, pick a dry fly that imitates an insect trout will recognize as food.

- Recognize the different rise forms of mayflies, caddisflies, midges, and other aquatic and terrestrial insects.

- When trout are rising all around, it is very difficult to take the time to find the seine and check for clues as to what the trout are rising to. Do it anyway. The seine will show you what the trout are feeding on—the river will tell you what to do.

- Never jump in wading and spraying your casts. Wade as little as possible, and keep a low profile. Wading spooks small fish upstream where they might alert larger trout. Wading also destroys trout spawning nests, upsets trout habitat, and kills aquatic insects.

- Get as close to rising trout as possible. You can get very close to trout from downstream, and it will keep you from casting into and across mixed currents to defeat drag. Wait for a few more rises—I call them confidence rises—and observe what insect and what stage it is taking. If searching the water during nonhatch times, get close to holding water before casting.

- Count the trout's rise rhythm, and if, for instance, the trout is feeding every four seconds, put your fly in front of it in four seconds, and if on still water, cast in front of the fish the same distance as between its past rises.

- If coming from upstream, don't send a wading wave or debris that would put the rising fish down, maybe for the day.

- Use a short, slack, pinpoint-accurate cast as fish work in very narrow feeding lanes and will not move far for a natural or for your fly. Do not false cast over the fish as they will see the line or be spooked by water drops.

- Longer casts result in bad presentation, and you lose track of the fly. It is always best to be patient and hold your fire rather than present a long cast and spook the fish.

- Watch your fly closely as it approaches the rising fish. Often, you will see the fish fin up and inspect your offering and then turn away.

If that is the case, it is important to rest the trout for a minute to allow it a confidence rise or two before presenting the fly again while paying greater attention to the drift of the fly. Drag must be avoided; it is usually the reason the fish didn't take the fly on the first cast.

- If there are several trout rising, pick one and concentrate on presenting an accurate cast to it. Don't spray casts among rising fish; that will certainly spook them.

- When trout are rising and the evening light is getting low and making it tough to see your fly, use a short cast and adjust your position in relation to the trout so you can keep track of your fly and rises to it.

- Dead drifting, twitching, high floating, and pulling a dry fly under the surface should all be tried and will, at times, entice some trout when all else fails.

- Wear earth-toned clothing to prevent unnatural contrast with natural surroundings.

- Do not give up. Trout may be sleeping. Yes, they do. If there is no hatch and every fly you try fails to bring fish up, take a break and return later.

Hilary Oliver catches and releases her first fish ever on the Fall River, Idaho. Is this fishing fun or what? *Photo: Jeremy Koreski*

The Young Leading the Old

Last summer I taught two very experienced spring creek anglers how to fish tenkara, but they struggled for an hour before picking it up. Both were typical of experienced anglers learning a new method. The men were quite honestly insecure, lacked confidence, and tended to overthink the simple and easy processes of tenkara. What turned the tide was when a six-year-old nephew of one of the men took my rod and began catching small trout on a grasshopper dry fly within minutes, much to the men's chagrin. Soon they both learned the proper dry fly tenkara technique from the six-year-old.

—Craig Mathews

Lola hooks another one. Fall River, Idaho. *Photo: Jeremy Koreski*

USEFUL DRY FLY PATTERNS

While there are thousands of effective dry fly patterns for fishing the various hatches and insects, the ones I list here are simple to tie and proven to catch big trout. This short list should prepare anglers for the entire year of dry fly fishing.

MAYFLY DUNS AND SPINNERS

We developed the Sparkle Dun pattern to imitate most emerging mayfly species. This fly in a few different sizes and colors will fill 95 percent of your mayfly fishing needs.

Yellow-Tan and Olive Sparkle Duns

>Hook: #12 to #20, dry fly
>
>Thread: 8/0 gray is a good neutral color for all Sparkle Dun types
>
>Tail (shuck): mayfly brown Zelon one-half to a full hook shank in length
>
>Body: to match naturals, yellow-tan and olive are most common
>
>Wing: natural deer hair

Note: All Sparkle Duns are tied in the same style; the differences are in size and body color to match natural insects.

Rusty and Olive Sparkle Spinners

>Hook: #12 to #20, dry fly
>
>Thread: 8/0 gray
>
>Tail: dun or cream hackle fibers
>
>Body: to match naturals, with rusty and olive the most common
>
>Wing: white Zelon tied spent, half spent, or upright

CADDISFLIES

The Iris and X2 Caddis patterns are very easy to tie and very effective.

Amber and Olive Iris Caddis

> Hook: #14 to #18, dry fly
>
> Thread: 8/0 gray
>
> Shuck: amber Zelon
>
> Body: amber or olive Zelon dubbing blend
>
> Wing: dun or white Zelon looped and tied low over body
>
> Head: hare's mask shaggy

X2 Caddis in Tan and Olive

> Hook: #14 to #18, dry fly
>
> Thread: 8/0 gray
>
> Shuck: amber Zelon
>
> Body: Zelon dubbing blend of olive or tan
>
> Rib: one strand of pearl Krystal Flash wrapped five times up the body
>
> Wing: natural deer hair

STONEFLIES

By having a few sizes and colors in your fly boxes, you are ready to fish stonefly activity.

Nick's Giant and Golden Sunken Stones

> Hook: #6 to #10, dry fly
>
> Thread: 6/0 to match body color
>
> Tail/egg sac: black poly yarn
>
> Body: orange Zelon dubbing for giant stone, yellow for golden stone
>
> Wings: five to seven clumps of deer hair

Little Yellow Stone Adult

> Hook: #12 to #16, dry fly
>
> Thread: 8/0 yellow
>
> Tag: red Zelon
>
> Body: little yellow stonefly Zelon dubbing blend
>
> Wing: yellow dyed elk or deer hair
>
> Hackle: grizzly or ginger

Zelon Midge

Hook: #20 and #22, dry fly

Thread: 8/0 gray

Shuck: dun Zelon

Body: thread wrapped over Zelon Shuck

Thorax: midge black Zelon dubbing blend

Wing: dun Zelon

Head: black Zelon dubbing blend

Griffith's Gnat

Hook: #16 to #20, dry fly

Thread: 8/0 gray

Body: two to three strands of peacock herl

Hackle: grizzly palmered through body, four to six wraps

Important fly patterns to have during summer months.

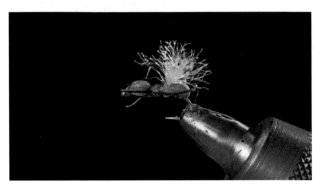

Blue and Olive Foam Damsels

Hook: #10, dry fly

Thread: 8/0 gray

Body: strip cut of closed-cell foam (or braided mono) in blue or olive

Wing: clear or white Medallion sheeting cut to shape, or white Zelon tied spent

Hackle: wraps of grizzly hackle in front of wings

Cinnamon and Black Zelon Flying Ants

Hook: #14 and #16, dry fly

Thread: 8/0 black

Body: closed-cell foam, black or cinnamon

Wings: white Zelon

Legs: fine black rubber legs

Blue and Red Foam Dragons

Same as above although red foam substituted for olive and cut strip of foam more robust to mimic that of dragonfly. No hackle needed.

Foam Bee

Hook: #14, dry fly

Thread: 8/0 black

Body: striped black and yellow foam body material

Wing: white Zelon

Hackle: grizzly

Black Foam Beetle

Hook: #14 and #16, dry fly

Thread: 8/0 black

Body: black dubbing, or omit

Shell (back): black closed-cell foam strip pulled over body

Legs: black round rubber legs

Indicator: orange closed cell foam

Head: butt of foam used for shell back

Black Foam Cricket

Hook: #10, dry fly

Thread: 6/0 black

Body: black closed-cell foam

Legs: black rubber legs

Indicator: bright orange yarn, or omit

Chaos Grasshopper

Hook: #12 and #14, dry fly

Thread: 6/0 brown

Body: tan closed-cell foam

Legs: yellow rubber legs and brown hackle (optional)

Indicator: orange closed-cell foam

Wing: pale yellow Zelon

Spruce Moth

Hook: #12, dry fly

Thread: 8/0 rusty dun

Body: amber Zelon dubbing blend

Wing: deer hair

OTHER USEFUL PATTERNS

There are a couple of useful dry fly patterns anglers may want to have for searching the waters during nonhatch periods.

Adams Cripple

Hook: #16, dry fly

Thread: 8/0 gray

Tail/Shuck: mayfly brown Zelon

Body: fine gray dubbing

Wing: white Zelon

Hackle: mixture of wraps of brown and grizzly

Royal Wulff Cripple

Hook: #14, dry fly

Thread: 8/0 black

Tail/Shuck: mayfly brown Zelon

Body: peacock herl and red floss

Wing: white Zelon

Hackle: brown

Sleeping Trout

Last winter we were doing some filming and wanted to get underwater footage of fish feeding on midge pupae before the hatch and fish rising to emerging midges. We arrived, set up, and tried every fly in our boxes before I asked the cameraman to put his tiny underwater camera on a long probe and search nearby rocks and pockets for fish. A minute later, he had me check out his viewfinder, and there was the proof: several trout sleeping next to boulders and logs. We had an early lunch, midges emerged, and the fish came out and fed; we got some nice filming in late that morning.

Another time, my friend Terry and I hiked into a secret lake only to find hundreds of big rainbows in a ball, slowly circling while sleeping along the lake's drop-off. Terry presented a heavily weighted nymph into the ball of trout to wake them up and took a huge rainbow on his first cast. A short while later, mayflies emerged and the fish rose to them; we had a banner day.

—Craig Mathews

Bull trout rest after a long migration. British Columbia. *Photo: Steven Gnam*

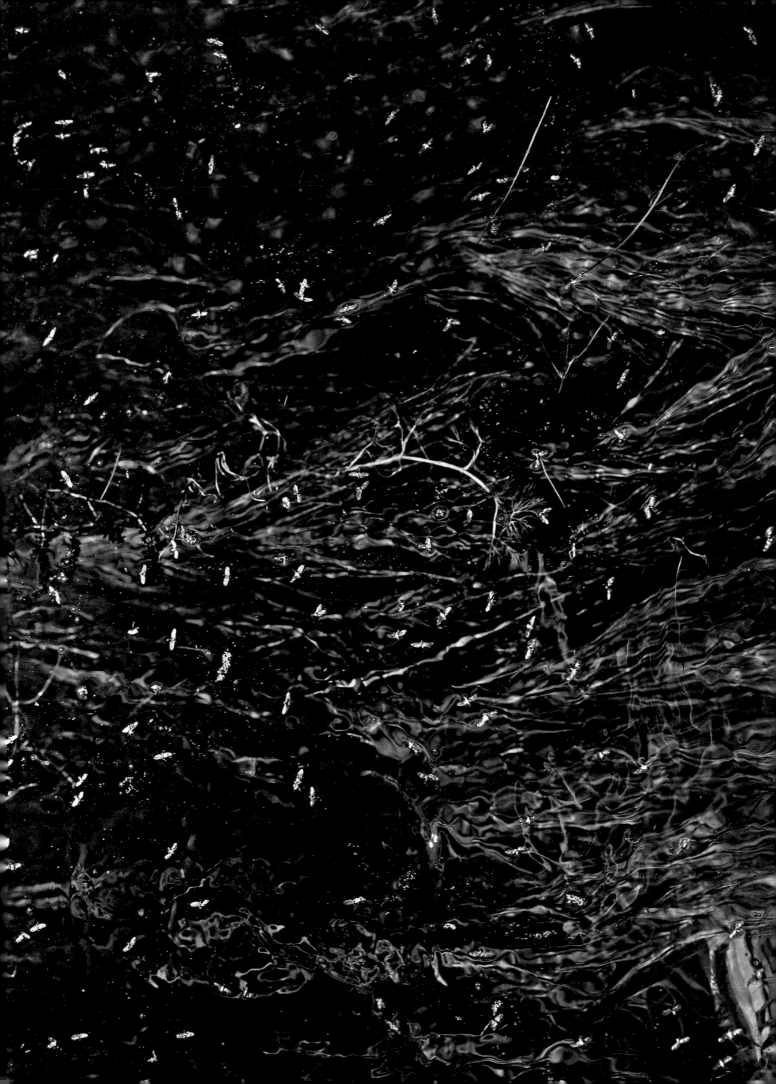

Chapter 5: Fishing Situations

YVON CHOUINARD, CRAIG MATHEWS, AND MAURO MAZZO

The fisher who declares that he or she fishes only with dry flies or nymphs or streamers or casts only to rising fish regardless of the conditions will often find himself or herself fishing in an ineffective way.

Certain rivers, or parts of rivers, can be fished most effectively with very specific techniques. When you add the season of the year, the time and conditions of the day, the insect activity at that hour, and so on, you have a puzzle that cannot be solved with a single technique.

However, there is no need for the average angler to be an entomologist. You need not know the difference between a mahogany dun nymph and a pale morning dun nymph. You can even forget about emergence dates, fly sex, maturity, and immaturity. You need not always have to match the hatch. Look at the water in front of you, break it down into segments, and think about where the fish are holding and where you need to be to present a fly to them: Develop a simple, effective plan.

Opposite: A trico hatch on the Henry's Fork spring creek. *Photo: Jeremy Koreski*

The Detective

Angling legend Charlie Brooks once said, "The single most important thing a fly fisher can know is the character and quality of the rivers and streams he or she fishes."

Three things often limit the success of anglers, beginners and experienced alike: trying to fish too much water in too little time, a lack of simple planning, and using inappropriate tools, methods, or techniques. Knowing what to expect on the rivers, lakes, and streams you plan to fish can save you time and money and result in huge successes. There is much fly fishing information available online, in books, at local fly shops, and from fly fishing guides and clubs. Armed with this information, anglers can be prepared to fish their target waters in most fishing situations.

Before you can catch fish, you have to know where the fish are and what they are eating. You have to do a little homework. You have to know what to expect and have an initial concept of when to switch from nymph to wet or to dry. Read books, research online, talk to those who know; find out what bugs to expect and the dates of emergence for those bugs for your target river. Bring a little net to find out what bugs are on the river when you get there. Look under rocks, around bushes, and in the air. Do what the river tells you to do.

– Craig Mathews

Craig Mathews reads the rocks. Madison River, Montana. *Photo: Patrick Daigle*

A fine westslope cutthroat from British Columbia's Elk River. *Photo: John Juracek*

The Innovator

I clearly remember the most memorable trout that I've ever caught. I had spotted a large Snake River cutthroat sipping pale morning duns (PMDs) on Flat Creek in Jackson Hole. I've found that cutthroats feeding on PMDs can be extremely selective, often keying in on only one stage of the mayfly.

This fish was feeding close to the cutbank of this meadow creek just below a little snag. It would take a delicate curve cast to the left to avoid the snag, and the best I could get would be a two-foot-long drift.

After countless tries, I finally started to get the cast down, but the clever fish had no interest in my dry fly. I cast and rested the fish and cast again for almost an hour. Finally, I put it all together with a combination of 7X tippet, a lucky curve cast, and a stripped-down size 20 PMD dry fly that I converted into a "physically challenged emerger." The final solution was to put spittle on the back third of the fly so it hung below the surface film. Don't be afraid to experiment; try different things, and figure out what works.

– Yvon Chouinard

The Fish

When I start fishing, I try to think like a fish or at least try to guess where a fish would stay and what it is going to do. I look around for likely places, like boulders, that offer good cover and a continual supply of food. For instance, you might think that the middle of a big pool in a sizeable river is the best place, but most of the time it is the worst; the middle of the pool is where the fish are more exposed to predators. You will find only small fish there, and we want to catch the big one.

The first places you want to look at are nice rocks at the tails of pools. Those are the first places I would stay if I were a fish. Going upstream, if I were a fish, I would hang under the edges of the current that is created by big boulders. On those edges a fish would certainly have larvae or insects drifting down with the current.

The best places for fish are ones that have plenty of cover. Nice big pocket water is the best place for the big fish to be and where they can find easy food. It's like having a holiday in Mexico: You lie down, wait for the food, and then go back to your beach chair. That's what fish want to do; fish are lazy.

– Mauro Mazzo

No need to hurry, it's a cripple. A native Yellowstone cutthroat rises for a green drake mayfly in the Yellowstone River, Yellowstone National Park, Montana. *Photo: John Juracek*

FAST MOUNTAIN WATERS

Turbulent water, to be sure, but plenty of trout live along the quiet edges of the Lamar River. This is ideal water for a heavy nymph. *Photo: John Juracek*

Rivers and streams that flow through canyons or gorges are usually rough-and-tumble waters. Most are rich in insect life. They tumble over boulders and jagged rocks and are hard or impossible to wade—and sometimes dangerous. Wade rough-and-tumble waters as little as possible to avoid a dunking.

In rough-and-tumble waters, trout need relief from heavy currents. Most first timers focus on the standing waves of white water as they crash around huge boulders and snags of timber. But anglers should disregard the rough water in the middle of the river and instead concentrate on the slower margins—the pockets and pools along the edges. Fish the river as you would a small trout stream.

Trout do not occupy every inch of a fast, rough stream or river. And they will not move far for a natural or artificial fly. It is important to fish only the holding water where fish are lying and accustomed to getting their groceries. Holding water also gives trout protection and security.

This type of water is the easiest to read and learn because of all the clues it offers: visible currents, foam lines, pockets, pools, seams, and obstructions like boulders and log jams. An added plus is the noise of the waves and heavy currents that allows fishers to get close to holding water without spooking fish.

Visible currents are created as water moves swiftly around boulders and waterfalls or as it whirlpools and bubbles behind downed timber. These currents are easy to see, and relief from them means big trout will be present—and usually lots of them.

Foam lines are apparent but are seldom recognized as the conveyer belt bringing food to, or providing escape routes for, trout. Thin foam lines appear behind or next to boulders in the main current or along boulders next to the bank where several currents may merge. Below this, the foam line spreads out, and at this point, in the broader and slower currents, trout begin to hold and feed. The foam lines must be six inches or wider before trout will use them for cover, feeding, and relief from heavy currents.

A pocket is deep water located below a logjam or boulder. Fish use pockets like they use foam lines.

Seams are the transition water most trout prefer to hold in. The water separating the quiet water on the inside from the fast water on the outside of boulders is a good example. There are seams on and beneath the surface. They may be associated with visible currents, pockets, undercuts, foam lines, or logjams. As anglers put in more time on the water, they will come to readily recognize more productive seams. Seams can be counted on to produce more good trout than any other area.

Jeremiah Watt negotiates the rough-and-tumble water of Big Cottonwood Creek, Utah. Photo: Jay Beyer

Davide rappelling down the Cascata del Tinaccio, on the Artogna River, Italy. *Photo: Mauro Mazzo*

The Journey Versus the Destination

Davide is a good friend who works as a Sesia riverkeeper. For years, he and I had been looking at a very big pool on a nearby river that was nearly impossible to reach. Above and below it were more than 150 feet of sheer rock wall. Because it was so hard to get to, we figured no one had fished it: We thought that a place like that should have plenty of fish and possibly some big ones.

One summer day, we decided it was high time to fish it, and we worked out a plan to reach the pool and gathered the necessary gear. We climbed up to the top of the sidewall, crossed it, rappelled down to the pool, and eventually fished the pool.

Since we thought this would be a day to remember, we decided to take lot of pictures. We started early in the morning, and while Davide climbed the correct side of the rock wall and rappelled down to the pool, I climbed the opposite side of the wall and took pictures of him as he reached the spot. Once he got close to the pool, he stopped and waited for me: The magic moment had to be shared.

So I rappelled down my side of the rock wall, climbed up the right side, and rappelled down again to join Davide. All this took about eight hours, but now we were there, ready to fish the pool that no one had ever fished before.

Davide insisted I had to fish it first. Eager to accept his graciousness, I tied a small nymph on, and as soon as the fly touched the water, I put a little tension on the line, anxious to feel the bite. Nothing. I cast again, waited a little bit more, and nothing. Next, Davide took a turn.

We tried just about every fly and every trick, but we did not get a single touch. We sadly came to the realization that there were no fish at all in the pool. Disappointed, we decided to leave.

We were silent on the way back home, each coming to grips with our failure. But after a while we started talking, and we agreed that although we didn't catch any fish the day was really fun, and we had learned a lesson: It is the journey that is important, not the destination.

– Mauro Mazzo

Wet Fly Fishing Fast Mountain Waters

Fast mountain streams are caddis and stonefly water; I wouldn't bother with small flies. This is good water to do the two-fly, soft hackle and dry caddis, technique. Use a large attractor soft hackle like a size 8 or 10 for the point fly and a large buoyant dry fly for the dropper.

Cast downstream so the point fly enters first into every piece of soft water, foam line, eddy, or pocket. Sometimes in rough water you can bounce the dropper fly off the top of little waves. If that doesn't result in a strike, drag the soft hackle upstream and into the same areas.

You can also run a streamer through these same places. If there is a suck hole or reversal, drop the streamer in it and the fly will get sucked down so you can get the fly down deeper into the next pocket.

— Yvon Chouinard

Nymph Fishing Fast Mountain Waters

Keep the casting to a minimum in this kind of water to avoid spooking fish. In very small pockets, do not cast at all, and just drop the fly right above the spot you want to fish.

The easiest way to fish the nymph in this kind of water is to use a tandem formed by a big dry fly and a lightly weighted nymph tied under the dry at a distance of about one and a half times the average depth of that stretch of water. The use of a speed dropper like the one Yvon describes in the wet fly tenkara section (page 51) will give you the opportunity to remove it quickly and switch back to fishing with only the one nymph when you find a deeper pool so you can fish it properly.

You will see some spots on a steep creek that look impossible to fish but often hold some big fish. The most common spot is the area under an overhanging tree with branches touching the water. An impossible place to cast to, but there is a solution—a dirty trick.

Walk upstream of the spot—preferably on the riverbank, not in the water—making the least noise possible. Position yourself about twenty-five feet upstream of the spot. Tie a big caddis on the dropper, and use a small weighted nymph as the point fly. Put the fly on the water, and shaking the rod tip, let out enough line so your rig gets under the branches. If there is a fish around, he will take it.

— Mauro Mazzo

In this clear limestone water the fish are hiding above and below rocks and in the deeper pools, coming out in the open only when there is an active hatch. Plan River, Alto Adige, Italy. *Photo: Mauro Mazzo*

Old School

One of the Valsesia's old fishing masters, Arturo Pugno, told me about a style of fishing where they tied a special rig made with three hooks and a dead fish on one of the hooks. Then they maneuvered it into the broken water under a cascade to give the marble trout the illusion of a wounded fish.

They were fishing with no reel, using heavy cane rods with a rope attached to the butt. When they hooked a fish that was really big, they threw the rod in the water and watched it until it got close to the bank, a sign that the fish was tired. If that didn't happen, they had to jump in the water and swim after it.

Arturo's biggest marble trout was more than fifteen pounds. After more than an hour, the fish was not coming close to the bank, and he decided to swim in the river, grab the rod, and pull the fish in. This was nothing unusual for him, except that it was February and the temperature was many degrees below freezing.

– Mauro Mazzo

The old ways die hard: Arturo Pugno, 'the Valsesiana master,' fishing with his sixty-year-old solid cane rod on the Sesia River, Italy. He spotted a good grayling in the fast current. *Photo: Mauro Mazzo*

DRY FLY FISHING FAST MOUNTAIN WATERS

When fishing dry flies, you want to be fishing rough-and-tumble waters when insect activity occurs. If you want to fish a caddis hatch, you should arrive late in the day as caddis emergences occur in the evenings. This is where planning for success is so important.

Slowly walk the banks and fish every hold, pocket, and seam. If you suspect trout will be rising to an expected hatch, walk well back from the banks to avoid disturbing the water.

If there is an emergence of caddis or mayflies, match it and fish accordingly. If no fish are rising and no insects are active, pick a fly that imitates an insect trout recognize as food for that time period.

On rough water, trout often appear to be rising to mayfly duns riding the surface. Pick a fish and present your cast while observing the fish. If the trout lets duns pass as it continues to rise in the holding water,

switch to an emerger or wingless floating fly or cut the wing off the dry fly you are using.

If fishing midges, anglers should keep in mind that trout working midges in rough-and-tumble conditions do so in thin water. They are very hard to approach and usually you will get only one drift over them. These fish are used to deep water with cover, heavy flows, and security, so try not to wade when getting close enough to present a cast.

The finest dry fly angling on rough-and-tumble waters occurs when female salmonflies return to the water to lay eggs during the afternoon. It is important to locate the area on the river when and where the females are laying their eggs to be successful.

– Craig Mathews

The Plan River is a very secluded place with almost no fishing pressure. Alto Adige, Italy. *Photo: Mauro Mazzo*

That Old Guy

Last summer, I watched four anglers fishing an area the size of a pool table for two hours on a rough-and-tumble water stretch of the Madison River. As I sat on the opposite side of the river fishing a caddis emergence, catching and releasing several trout, I noted they were not taking a single fish. I knew why. The water they presented their flies in was six inches deep and very swift, not the water trout would hold or feed in. Still, the anglers cast and cast and switched positions several times.

The next day, I saw their vehicle as it pulled up in front of our shop. The four young anglers strolled into the store, and I asked how their fishing had been. They said they'd just pulled in late yesterday from a marathon drive all the way from Atlanta, Georgia, and had fished the night before but had not taken a fish. They said something about an old guy across the river from them taking fish last night. I could not resist and told them "that old guy was me." I gave the red-faced newbies a few Iris Caddis emergers and drew them a map of where to expect rising fish near the Three Dollar Bridge along the Madison.

The next morning, they came in with fresh coffee and a donut for "the old guy," thanking me for showing them where to fish during evening caddis on rough water like the Madison River.

– Craig Mathews

The "old guy" at his tying desk. Blue Ribbon Flies, West Yellowstone, Montana. *Photo: Patrick Daigle*

SLOW MEADOW WATERS

On a meadow or spring creek the larger fish are holed up under the undercut banks. South Fork of the Madison, Montana.
Photo: John Juracek

This water type is typically a meandering meadow stream with even, smooth currents interspersed with riffles and pools. Reading this water requires lots of bank walking, concentration, great eyesight, and plenty of patience, but it also may provide a few pleasant surprises like huge trout rising to the surface that leave barely a dimple.

Beginning anglers should also be on the watch for fish migration on slow meadow waters. An area that fishes well one day may be devoid of trout the next. Some feel that fish do not adopt a permanent holding spot on slow meadow waters. On many smooth rivers and streams, it pays to move and cover lots of water if you fail to raise fish in spots where you had recently found them.

Sound and vibrations transmit very far on these meadow creeks. You need to walk very quietly to avoid spooking these fish. You really should be barefooted or wearing leather moccasins.

There are four features found on slow meadow waters that concentrate insects and trout rising to them. You should watch for whirlpools, back currents, scum lines, and feeding troughs.

Whirlpools are formed when currents work

around logs, sweepers, and islands. Look for back currents that collect insects at the end of whirlpools. Be alert here for single trout, and whole pods, that will come to the surface for terrestrial imitations like ants, bees, grasshoppers, and crickets as well as insect emergences of mayflies and caddis. Due to the direction of flow in whirlpools and back currents, trout may face downstream.

Scum lines and feeding troughs are found where currents come together. Slow meadow waters hold areas where one current sweeps along an overhanging bank as another current comes off a weed bed or obstruction like a log and merges with it at a gravel ledge. These scum lines provide tight feeding lanes, and trout will seldom move far to take a fly. In places like this, trout might drop back to where two scum lines come together to form a longer, wider lane known as a feeding trough. The troughs might be several feet wide and several feet long and hold dozens of trout.

Other excellent places are the potential shelters close to the bank. Undercut banks and logs and stones breaking the current along the bank create ideal habitat for fish. Also search the pocket water created by a stone or a log breaking the water's flow midstream. The fish will often hold in this calm water, feeding on the two currents in which the main current has been split by the obstruction. Check also for any deeper and slower stretches.

The long evenings of June provide plenty of time for fishing on the Madison River in Yellowstone Park. *Photo: John Juracek*

Wet Fly Fishing Slow Meadow Waters

Soft hackles will work whenever there is a bit of depth (more than six inches) and moving water. You will catch mostly small fish in the shallow water except in the early mornings or evenings when there can be some larger fish.

Inside every bend of the stream, there will be a deep pool. That's where the big fish are, tucked down deep under the undercut banks. They don't like to come out for anything small or that isn't at their depth. In the evenings, fish with heavy streamers to draw out these big brown or brook trout.

– Yvon Chouinard

Nymph Fishing Slow Meadow Waters

The prime waters for the nymph fishers here are the undercut banks and the deeper waters.

Undercut banks are some of the most interesting water on a small stream; these are the places where the big guys hide. Here, your chances of success depend on the way you approach the stream. The noise made by your walking will scare the fish, so you have to move either like a ballet dancer or a special-forces member. They are quite different people, but both of them are really good at moving lightly; choose the style that suits your personality.

You will need to fish either at short or medium distance. If you are able to see the nymph in the water, short-distance sight fishing will be your choice. Cast as close to the bank as possible and follow the drift of your fly with your eyes. If you see anything happening close to your fly, like a sudden flash or a shadow covering the fly, strike. Often, that flash or shadow is a fish. If you have a problem seeing the fly or if the water is colored, use an indicator made with a piece of fluorescent nylon, or use a dry fly as an indicator.

There are strike indicators that look like a small float that you can buy in a fly fishing shop, but consider that the bigger the indicator, the more takes you will miss. This happens for two reasons. Very often, the fish takes the fly and spits it back out very quickly because it realizes there is something wrong; in this case, you will not even see the smallest movement in the float. The second reason is connected to this first. The resistance offered from the strike indicator to the nymph affects its drift and will increase the chances that the fish realizes there is something wrong and refuses your fly completely.

It is better yet to use a dry fly as an indicator. Working a nymph suspended to a dry fly will make it much more effective to fish the undercut banks: The fly will pass in front of the nose of the fish at the fish's depth, and you will be able to fish at longer distances, thereby reducing the chances of spooking the fish. Cast as close to the bank as possible and follow the drift of your fly with your eyes. If you see your indicator stop, strike immediately.

As a general rule, remember that we are trying to make a fish believe that a bunch of hair, fur, and feathers is real food. We should feel obliged to present it with the most natural drift. Otherwise we would be shameless.

If you are fishing a pool, the first place to look will be its head, where the food taken by the current settles down. Normally, there are also fish at the tails of the pools, but because the water is often shallower there, it is a better spot for the wet or dry fly fisher.

More often than not, it is mandatory to fish upstream, so the most effective technique will be high-stick nymphing. Keep your leader pretty short when fishing with a regular fly fishing rod and reel; you want to keep as much fly line as possible out of the tip to load the rod more easily. A good compromise for the leader is seven to eight feet with a tippet length of two feet.

Most of the time, one nymph will be sufficient, but if you like fishing tandems, the combination of a nymph and a dry fly can be very efficient. You can try the two-nymphs rig only in a very deep pool, where the use of a heavy nymph as point fly will help you reach the bottom quickly. Tie on a smaller fly as the dropper to differentiate the offer.

– Mauro Mazzo

DRY FLY FISHING SLOW MEADOW WATERS

Slow meadow waters always appear inviting and easy to fish with trout holding in every bend, but their gentle character belies their fickle nature. Here, the fish will not allow as close an approach as those trout rising in rough water. And myriad currents make drag a constant consideration. Make your cast and watch carefully as the fly approaches a rising fish.

If you see a trout holding, but not rising, try a beetle, ant, or bee straight upstream or slightly across and up. Limit your cast to not more than twenty-five feet. Usually, the fish will come up and take on your first or second offering. Often, it may inspect the fly on the first cast, then move back to its hold. Don't pick your fly off the water too quickly, as many times the fish will come back from its hold and take the fly. If you had pulled your fly off the water, the trout returning to search for it might spot you and spook, or the fish might become suspicious and refuse to look at your next presentation.

When fishing dry caddis patterns on slow meadow water, approach from upstream and cast across and slightly downstream. If you have to approach from downstream, present your fly on a slightly up-and-across angle.

In summer, with so many other insects emerging on smooth flowing waters, many anglers fail to consider midges when they come upon rising trout. There are times, however, when fish will take only impaired or crippled adult midges, even though there may be far more caddis or mayflies present on the water.

Use terrestrial patterns to prospect slow meadow waters. A favorite method on slow meadow waters is to walk the high banks and bluffs of rivers and streams and every few yards creep to the edge of sharp banks and bluffs that overlook the river. You will be amazed at how many fish are in knee-deep water waiting on terrestrials to fall, crawl, or fly into the water. Fish searching for terrestrials will travel considerable distances, so it is always best to have someone watch the fish while the other sneaks up from downstream: It's of no use casting to where a fish was instead of where it is.

– Craig Mathews

Feedlines, rocks, and deep depressions equal ideal trout water. The Gallatin River in Yellowstone Park. *Photo: John Juracek*

Fooled by Midges

My good friend Terry and I were fishing the Firehole River last spring during epic pale morning dun and caddis emergences. Fish were feeding everywhere along the meadow stretches of the river. We walked to the river and sat on the bank, excited by so many fish we thought were feeding on emerging PMDs or caddis. Instead of taking time to carefully observe the river and determine what the fish were feeding on, we rigged up—Terry with a caddis emerger and I with a PMD mayfly cripple. Several minutes and no fish later, we sloshed to the shore and took out our handy insect nets to sample the flow. There we saw what the river was telling us to do; in the tiny mesh of our insect nets were dozens of midge emergers, many crippled and impaired. We knotted on Zelon midges and each took several rising fish that morning.

– Craig Mathews

Dawn patrol: Streamer fishing for fall-run brown trout on the upper Madison River, Montana. *Photo: John Juracek*

SPRING CREEKS

Spring creeks are rich with aquatic plants and insects. Idaho. *Photo: Steven Wohlwender*

Spring creeks offer the most challenging fly fishing opportunities. They feature constant, clear flows in mixed currents over weed banks and obstructions. To get to know one is to spend much time on its waters. They are often moody and changing, and anglers must adapt to be successful.

Spring creek trout are usually visible as they actively feed on insect activity like emergences and egg-laying times. Look for fish to be holding in or near weed banks, overhangs, undercuts, downed trees, and brush as well as under bridges. It pays to be patient and spend time observing and sneaking along at a snail's pace learning the creek and its secrets.

Wet Fly Fishing Spring Creeks

One of the largest spring creeks in the world is the Henry's Fork of the Snake River in Idaho. With its slow-moving water, complex micro-currents created by weed beds, and multiple and complex hatches, it is one of the most challenging streams to fish. Consequently, it attracts some of the best fly fishermen from all over the world.

When there is a hatch happening, it is best to try to match the exact insect, stage, and even gender of the bug that you think they are feeding on. When there are fish rising but there are no visible bugs around, you can often induce the take by fishing a soft-hackle Partridge and Pheasant Tail, which imitates most mayflies.

Cast downstream to the rising fish, except in the summer when floating pieces of grass make it impossible to swing wet flies. In conditions like this, I position myself across from the fish and fish the soft hackle dead drifted like a nymph or emerger. Use only one fly because with a fish on, the other fly will catch on weeds or grass.

The micro-currents that are the bane of the dry fly purist are not a bother with my soft hackle. Also, since I am fishing downstream and the fish never sees my tippet, I don't have to use 6X or 7X tippets, an advantage when landing one of those hefty rainbows.

This is just one example of where the wet fly technique excels on spring creek water.

– Yvon Chouinard

Nymph Fishing Spring Creeks

More often than not, it is mandatory to fish upstream and quite far from the fish, in order not to be seen. For this reason, sight fishing at a medium to long distance is the tactic to use. Long leaders are mandatory, together with a very delicate presentation; you want to disturb the water as little as possible.

It is better to use only one nymph, because when sight fishing it is difficult enough to follow the drift of one fly, let alone two. The most effective way to cover this kind of water is to cast a small mayfly imitation up and across to rising fish. I would suggest a Pheasant Tail Nymph tied on a size 16 or 18 hook as universal fly. If you see anything happening close to your fly, like a sudden flash or a shadow covering the fly, strike.

– Mauro Mazzo

One of the world's largest spring creeks, the Railroad Ranch section of the Henry's Fork, Idaho. *Photo: Jeremy Koreski*

Dry Fly Fishing Spring Creeks

Because spring creeks are so challenging to dry fly fish, successful anglers must be prepared to fish predictable insect activity. Know the weather forecast for the day you are fishing: Cool, damp days provide optimal conditions for heavy mayfly hatches.

Blind fishing a spring creek when there are no rising trout only spooks the fish and is seldom productive. There are exceptions such as during terrestrial periods when grasshoppers, beetles, ants, and butterflies are active; the other is during damselfly and dragonfly periods. This might be the only time anglers see big trout throw caution to the wind and chase natural and artificial flies.

On smaller spring creeks, you seldom need to wade, and if you do, it is only to get into position for a cast. On large spring creeks, you often have to wade to follow fish rising to insects as they move upstream. Always approach rising trout from downstream and present casts to them up and across.

– Craig Mathews

Jiry Klima, one of the most successful Czech competition fishermen, nymphing on the Vltava River, Czech Republic.
Photo: Mauro Mazzo

FREESTONE RIVERS AND STREAMS

Typical freestone water on a northern section of the Sesia River, Italy. *Photo: Mauro Mazzo*

There are few surprises on freestone waters; they are read like an open book, with trout holding where they should in pockets and pools or at the bottom of riffles and runs. There are always plenty of overhangs, undercuts, sweepers, and rock piles. They include the habitats covered already in the sections on fast mountain and slow meadow waters. And big freestone rivers can be broken down into those fishing situations.

When no insects are bringing fish to the surface on freestone waters, search for trout in riffles, runs, pockets, pools, sweepers, and overhangs. These waters are always cold and some of the last to clear of snowmelt. Insect emergences are later than those on larger waters that warm earlier. Hatches are unpredictable due to late snows or erratic spring weather. All this can make planning to fish them difficult.

Deep Knowledge

We've heard a story about a young Native American fellow in Oregon who decided he wanted to become a steelhead guide. For a couple of days, he floated down the river with a mask and snorkel observing where the fish were. He immediately became the best guide on the river. What he observed in a couple of days would take years and millions of casts to learn in the normal way.

– Yvon Chouinard

Claire Chouinard swims with the sockeye. Adams River, British Columbia. *Photo: Matt Stoecker*

Wet Fly Fishing Freestone Rivers

The techniques described in the chapter on fishing tenkara with soft hackles apply perfectly to freestone rivers.

If there is no specific hatch on, I would use a size 14 attractor pattern, find some moving water, and work my way downstream. Even if there is a hatch of midges or small mayflies, I often disregard the hatch and stick to an attractor fly. Even during the height of a salmonfly occurrence, I've been known to continue with a size 14 blue soft hackle . . . and catch my share of rainbows and browns.

– Yvon Chouinard

Nymph Fishing Freestone Rivers

A freestone river is essentially a bigger mountain stream, and most of the fishing situations are the same. Do not be misled by the dimension of the river; remember that fish are often close to the banks. Don't concentrate only on that pocket in the middle of the river that is impossible to reach; the fish are very often very close to your feet, and if they are not there, it is only because you scared them away. Described below are two situations that are unique to freestone rivers. One is a long run of water with a constant depth, and the other is a big pool with a dimension that can often confuse the novice.

A long run of water with a medium current and a depth of two to three feet is prime water for grayling in Europe. Locating the best spots when fish are rising is quite easy, but when there is no surface activity, this water can be difficult to read.

You have to remember that fishing nymphs is an exercise that involves reading the river in three dimensions, not two. So in this kind of water, you will have to look for any submerged rock or any variations of depth that can create a food deposit for the fish. Another indicator to use is the color of the bottom. Dark rocks covered with algae mean a mature bottom, a place where water always flows and where the algae offers perfect habitat for larvae and nymphs. A bottom made of sand or very light and clean rocks means poor habitat or a place that gets dry often—in other words, a place that offers no food.

Once you have located a nice-looking area, the best way to fish it is the classic Czech nymph way—fishing downstream with a short line. Fish the whole width of the river, moving toward the far bank; then walk downstream about ten feet, and come back fishing in the opposite direction.

Another way to cover this water while reducing the chances of scaring the fish—especially when the trout population is predominant—is to fish with a strike indicator. The drawbacks of this technique are discussed in the section on slow meadow water nymphing.

When fishing a big pool with a cascade at the head a good approach is to start from the tail, where usually you will find smaller fish. The water will be quite shallow, so use either two light nymphs or a dry fly and a nymph. My favorite rig is with a dry fly on the dropper, and a nymph as point fly, with about two feet between them.

The dry fly should be highly visible—I am devoted to a Klinkhammer fly, but a parachute fly also works. For the nymph, I suggest the always-effective #14 Pheasant Tail Nymph or Hare's Ear Nymph.

For the deep part of the pool, you can switch the small nymph to the dropper and tie on a heavier nymph as point fly. For this kind of rig, it is advisable to include a piece of fluorescent nylon in your leader to help detect the bite.

Once you are done with the deep part of the pool, you can proceed to fish the head of the pool. This is the most frightening water for a novice as the fast whitewater looks nearly unfishable, but this water often holds the biggest fish. Here you have only one choice: a big and heavy nymph. When fishing a nymph in whitewater, or under a fall, you first have to look for the slower current into which the main current is always broken and fish there.

Do not even try to make a free dead drift; more often than not you will snag your fly. Keep in mind that your fly always has to be kept under control. A way to fish this water is to use a big stonefly nymph and, keeping some tension on the line, let your fly sink till you feel the bottom. Then do a little twitch, to make the fly bounce on the bottom and to avoid snagging.

The best hook to use is a jig, as it works upside down and reduces the chance of snagging the fly on the bottom. The use of big flies, with bodies wrapped with turns of hackles, or made of bulky materials such as dubbed hare's ear, will also reduce the chances of snagging your fly on the bottom.

– Mauro Mazzo

DRY FLY FISHING FREESTONE RIVERS

Anglers should always have a few high-floating dry flies for searching this type of water. Bring a basic selection of mayflies, caddis, and stoneflies to imitate those you expect to find. Bring a small selection of terrestrials too. Work upstream and present a short, slack-line cast with a dead drift.

An effective method when approaching risers this closely is called "dapping." Sneak along the bank and keep a low profile while searching for the deepest, outside part of a meander. This is perfect for tenkara as, without casting, you can dap only your fly, tippet, and leader on the water in front of a rising fish.

On this water type, you will find many fish rising in each pool and pocket during mayfly activity. If you are fishing trout rising to a mayfly emergence, position yourself ten to fifteen feet below the rising trout and observe what the fish are rising to, and then present a pinpoint-accurate cast. These trout will rise in very narrow feeding lanes, so you must be on target.

On freestone rivers, pick a high-floating, visible caddis pattern that requires little babysitting to keep it floating. An X Caddis is easy to see, floats like a cork, and imitates an impaired or crippled caddis, a stage the trout recognize and take readily.

Stoneflies are usually present on all freestone waters, and you should be prepared to fish stonefly patterns whenever trout are rising to naturals.

But nothing compares to a late-summer day fishing terrestrials on freestone streams. As winter approaches, trout are willing to take most any terrestrial pattern, from butterflies to bees and crickets to grasshoppers. Fish the edges and overhangs where trout expect to see insects that have fallen into the water. Search all holding water, feeding lanes, seams, and pockets on a short line with a drag-free presentation. Don't spend too much time, though, as there will be a beaver dam or spring creek-like section of the freestoner just around the next bend with big trout rising.

– Craig Mathews

The Plan River, Alto Adige, Italy. *Photo: Mauro Mazzo*

New Year's Day

It was New Year's Day, and the morning temperature broke the plus side of zero for the first time in two weeks. A herd of elk grazed below the house near the river. Since the cold had kept us inside for so long, we decided we would head to the river to see if we could catch our first trout of the New Year.

There was no wind, and the sun was blinding as it burned off the hoarfrost on grasses along the river. We put on our pac boots, grabbed our tenkara rods, and slogged through several inches of snow to the river.

Midges were already emerging along the shore, and clusters of mating midges the size of dimes were rolling through holding water behind boulders and in pockets and pools. We watched several nice trout rise casually to midge clusters and took turns catching a few rainbows before the sun's rays lost their punch and midge activity shut down for the day.

– Craig Mathews

Midges are an important source of food for trout during the winter months; their emergences and egg laying often take place at temperatures at or even below freezing. *Photo: John Juracek*

LAKES AND PONDS

A typical alpine lake, best fished in the early morning or early evening when there is a hatch. Profa Lake, Santa Caterina Valfurva, Italy. *Photo: Mauro Mazzo*

Lakes, ponds, and sloughs will give the fly fisher opportunities to catch larger trout on flies on public water than any other water type.

When searching lakes for fish, look for drop-offs, weed beds, points of land extending into the lake, gravel bars and sandbars, and springs entering, as well as outlets leaving, the lake. Overhanging trees and downed timber provide good food sources and security areas for trout, and sagebrush banks and meadow areas along shorelines can bring grasshoppers, ants, and beetles to the water for fish to feed on. Remember, too, that the largest fish will be near the best security cover.

Trout in lakes are usually on the move as they look for food and the best cover, whereas trout in ponds and sloughs will often be stationary, facing into currents caused by springs or the dammed stream that forms the pond. Always slowly walk the bank, and use waterside cover to locate cruising fish. Be on the water at different times of the day in order to learn when and where the fish move and where their security areas are.

It pays to patiently walk the banks, staying well back from the shoreline. Use the sun to your advantage when stalking the banks for fish. You will be amazed how well trout stand out in sunlight. Nervous water created by fish moving and patrolling for food is a key for anglers to cast well in front of the wakes and strip a streamer or twitch a dry fly on their approach.

Anglers can also fish still waters by wading or from float tubes, boats, and small pontoon boats that are so popular now.

Locals Only

I will never forget locating the secret "locals" pond in Yellowstone with Labrador-sized brook trout. I was still police chief in West Yellowstone, and Larry, the town's attorney, had hinted its location to me that summer. When cop matters quieted in September, my wife, Jackie, and I headed out one frosty fall morning to find the pond he told me about that reportedly held four- to five-pound brook trout. We'd sloshed a couple of miles through beaver-dammed backwaters along a smooth-flowing stream where the tiny pond was hinted to be. Resting at a small spring inlet pond dammed by beavers, I told Jackie we had gone far enough and had to go back to Larry for more clues. Just then, three huge brook trout, as if on cue, jumped simultaneously not ten feet in front of us. It turned out we didn't need to go back to Larry; we had found the pond after all.

– Craig Mathews

The shallow, still waters of a beaver pond require a stealthy approach, long delicate leaders, and a "soft" presentation. Idaho.
Photo: John Juracek

Wet Fly Fishing Lakes and Ponds

Many lakes have leeches, which can be a primary food for lake-dwelling trout. Cast out, let them sink, and fish them with a slow strip with a pause in between strips. The fly needs to have an undulating motion like a swimming leech. Make sure your leech patterns have weight in the front.

All lakes have chironomids (midges), and a soft-hackle midge pattern fished with a twitch is a very effective technique as midges are very active swimmers. At a high-altitude lake in Wyoming, I've watched golden trout come up from twenty feet down to take a size 22 red-body soft hackle on the surface fished in this manner.

If there are caddis, a twitched soft-hackle caddis pattern will be more effective than a dead-drifted floating dry fly.

If there is not much going on insect-wise, try using two flies on light tippets, the point fly being a heavy bead head. Let them sink for as long as you can stand it, and then bring them up to the surface in small strips.

– Yvon Chouinard

Nymph Fishing Lakes and Ponds

When nymph fishing in lakes, it is imperative to scout around for the places described at the beginning of this section on lakes and ponds. If the wind is blowing, the downwind side of the lake or pond is usually the best, as most of the food will be taken there by the action of the wind. The use of two or three nymphs will cover more water.

When using a scud imitation, fish it with a nearly still line. Cast your flies as far as possible and let them reach the bottom; then do a little twitch every once in a while to make them more visible to the fish.

When fishing damselfly nymphs or other swimming nymphs, I suggest another approach, which is very useful when using intermediate or sinking lines. When the flies hit the water, count to five (one hundred and one, one hundred and two, etc.)—as a way of knowing what depth you reached—before starting a steady retrieve. If you get a take, you can reproduce that depth on the next cast. If you don't get a take, on the next cast count to seven or eight; repeat increasing the count until you discover the depth where the fish are. Then carry on fishing at this depth, varying only the retrieve.

– Mauro Mazzo

Dry Fly Fishing Lakes and Ponds

If you want to fish dry flies, be prepared for mayflies, midges, caddis, terrestrials, and damselflies and dragonflies. Be on the water when these insects are active, and they might bring trout to the surface. Few anglers try mice patterns on still waters. Dry mice flies can bring surface action at times, particularly in late evening and into the darkest hours.

On occasion, searching these waters with dry flies can be productive even though no insect activity is bringing trout to the surface. Try terrestrials along brushy banks or areas where overhanging trees bring ants, beetles, bees, or grasshoppers to the water.

If fishing from a float tube or boat, anglers must make sure not to create waves from the boat or float tube by kicking into position. Keep false casting to a minimum, and make sure your presentation is spot on target, as a rising fish will not move from its lane to take a fly.

At all times when fishing a caddis hatch, I use an impaired caddis adult with a trailing shuck like an X or X2 Caddis that floats and skitters well. Cast this dry fly in front of rising fish and strip it into their path with a six- to twelve-inch strip.

On lakes and ponds, midges bring up more trout than any other insect and should be at the top of your list when you see rising trout on still water. Most midge activity occurs during the warmest time of the day when it is calm, which is late afternoon around 6 p.m. Use a crippled or impaired midge adult or an emerging pupa, and get within thirty to thirty-five feet of the rising fish; obviously, you need to use a rod and reel for this type of fishing.

Big trout rising to midges often connect rises every few feet and are those fish that will respond best to proper presentations. They will lock into a feeding rhythm and take adults every few feet. Many times, you will see packs or pairs of fish traveling like wolves and feeding on crippled adult midges caught in their shucks—easy prey. Competition enters in as trout race to the naturals; it is the only time flock shooting works, as you are most certain to get a hit. Present your cast in the path of the rising fish; strike gently to protect your 6X tippet.

One other thing to remember is that after casting it is important to allow enough time to slowly pull on the line to remove slack in the tippet, forcing the fly to come around and face your position. If you fail to do this, the fly will drag even in still water.

– Craig Mathews

Hebgen Lake, Montana. *Photo: John Juracek*

Sam's First Fish

Late last summer, I was working with a couple of youngsters learning to fish tenkara. We were on a small meadow slough in Yellowstone just off the main road to Old Faithful. I could teach casting techniques to the kids on this tiny pond without concern for wind, brush, or overhanging trees. I knotted on a small grasshopper pattern after cutting the hook point off below the barb for safety. Sam made his first cast ever, a ten footer, against the shoreline, and I told him to twitch the fly then let it sit. He did, and immediately the fly was engulfed in a big swirling rise. I yelled as he yanked back hard on the rod. Since the hook had no point, the fish was gone. Sam asked, "What happened?" All I could offer was, "A big fish hit your fly."

I tied on a fly with a point and the barb mashed down. Sam made another cast, this time a twelve footer. The fly landed with a splat against the shoreline. I told him to twitch it a couple of times, then let it sit still. After a minute, I asked Sam to give the line a short tug. He began to pull the fly, and before it traveled a foot, a fourteen-inch brown slammed it. After a short run and two jumps, Sam towed the fish in, it being no match for 3X tippet. I have a photo of Sam, sporting a toothpaste grin and the fish.

– Craig Mathews

Fish on for seven-year-old Jack. Fall River, Idaho. *Photo: Jeremy Koreski*

Afterword

YVON CHOUINARD

The state of the art in angling these days is defined by "sports" standing in a guided drift boat mindlessly throwing Chernobyl ants at the bank. Or maybe just drifting along staring at the red-and-white bobber while the guide rows them into position. The next big advance will be fiber optics embedded in our lines so we can sit in the boat and watch a screen to know when to set the hook. If you didn't see it on your smartphone, did it really happen?

Angling doesn't have to drift further to the dark side. What's happened with fly fishing is no different from what's happened with every other sport or pastime—in fact, with society as a whole.

We all know the present world economy based on endlessly consuming and discarding is destroying our planet. We are the guilty ones. We are the consumers who "use up and destroy." We constantly buy things we want but don't need. And it seems we never have enough.

Our trout rods are designed to throw lead-weighted streamers clear across the river. Reels come with drags engineered to stop a truck, even though we know any old click drag will stop a trout. We love our tools, but too often they have become overbuilt and automated. They get between the user and the real experience.

The satisfaction to be gained from the synergy of hand, eye, and muscle are missing. When you have put in 10,000 hours to master a craft or sport, the Zen master would say, "Now see if you can accomplish the same without all the stuff."

In these trying times, when we are seeing the results of our high-tech, high-risk, and highly toxic economic system, many of us are questioning our frenetic consumer lifestyles. We yearn for a simpler life based not on refusing all technology, but on going back to appropriate technology, what David Brower describes as "turning around and taking a forward step."

It's difficult to imagine an economy that satisfies all seven billion of us, yet doesn't destroy the Earth. As it stands now, we are using up the resources of one and a half planets—a consumption level that is far from sustainable. And yet by 2050, that level is projected to rise to somewhere between three and a half and five planets. It seems we are doomed to endlessly recycle failed systems hoping that this time it will work. If repeating the same action and expecting a different outcome is one definition of insanity, where does that leave us? Certainly, we should replace old inefficient and polluting technology with less damaging and cleaner ones, but that does not solve the true problem: ever-expanding growth on a finite planet.

Just because society is hell-bent on becoming so complex that we finally snooker ourselves into a corner with all our stuff, it doesn't mean we have to go there. We can turn around and take that forward step.

We know we need to consume less on this finite planet. Yet if we do, it puts people out of work. But then with automation, robots, and technology there may not be very many jobs anyway. Perhaps if we buy only what we need rather than what we desire, and if we make sure that what we do buy is multifunctional, durable, repairable, high in quality, and won't go out of style—and can last long enough to be given to the next generation—then perhaps we can keep some people working.

I know there will always be work for the craftsman who spends forty hours making a beautiful and functional cane rod. And I can think of examples where the old ways of doing things have not been surpassed by modern technology.

Consider the "green revolution" farmer in his air-conditioned tractor producing inferior and even toxic food. Contrast that with the small organic farmer or gardener finding contentment and pleasure in using his hand tools or walking behind his perfectly trained plow horses or oxen. The "green revolution" is dependent on unsustainable chemical farming and actually produces less food per acre per resource investment over time.

I have friends who surf on replicas of eighteenth-century wooden surfboards from the Bishop Museum in Hawai'i. These surfboards are thin and flat as an ironing board with no fin, yet my friends ride them better than 99 percent of the surfers on modern plastic boards.

The professional load carriers around the world all carry loads on their heads, from African women with huge jars of water to Sherpa's who carry double loads (one hundred and ten pounds) with a tumpline. In fact, the United Nations conducted a study proving that carrying loads in these traditional ways is 50 percent more efficient than using a high-tech modern backpack.

The ship's carpenter on Shackleton's lifeboat the *James Caird* took only three simple hand tools with him on the passage from Antarctica to South Georgia Island, knowing if he needed to, he could build another boat with only those tools.

I believe the way to mastery of any endeavor is to work toward simplicity; replace complex technology with knowledge. The more you know, the less you need. In the 1980s, we used to say, "He who dies with the most toys wins." We were wrong.

The lesson we learn from fishing with a tenkara rod is that we shouldn't fear that a simpler life will be an impoverished life. Rather, simplicity leads to a richer and more satisfying way of fishing—and more importantly, living.

A selection of Bob Clay's hand built cane rods. *Photo: Tim Davis*

There are over 800,000 dams worldwide with hundreds of thousands that are silted in, obsolete, and damaging to people and the environment (40,000 in the United States alone). If you believe they should come down, start with the ones in your neighborhood. Matilija Dam, California. *Photo: Ben Knight*

Additional Resources

Short demonstration videos by each author covering basic tenkara techniques for wet flies, nymphing, and dry flies, plus basic setup of the rod, are available at www.patagonia.com/simpleflyfishing.

SUGGESTED READING

If you want to master angling with a fly, this is not the only book you need. Below are a few books we recommend on technique. There are many more: enough for a lifetime of inspiration.

- *Caddisflies*, Gary LaFontaine, Lyons Press, 1989
- *The Curtis Creek Manifesto*, Sheridan Anderson, Frank Amato Publications, 1978
- *Fly Casting Fundamentals*, Lefty Kreh, Stackpole Books, 2012
- *The Fly Fishers Craft*, Darrel Martin, Lyons Press, 2006
- *Reading Trout Water*, Dave Hughes, Stackpole Books, 2010
- *The Soft Hackled Fly and Tiny Soft Hackles*, 2nd ed., Sylvester Nemes, Stackpole Books, 2006
- *Trout Fishing*, Joe Brooks, Harper Row, 1972
- *Tying & Fishing Soft Hackled Nymphs*, Allen McGee, Frank Amato Publications, 2007
- *Western Fly-Fishing Strategies*, Craig Mathews, Lyons Press, 2007
- *Wet Flies*, Dave Hughes, Stackpole Books, 1995

RODS, LINES, FLIES, AND GEAR

- Blue Ribbon Flies, www.blue-ribbon-flies.com
- Patagonia, www.patagonia.com
- Temple Fork Outfitters, www.templeforkflyrods.com
- Tenkara USA, www.tenkarausa.com

The above companies are members of 1% for the Planet (except Temple Fork Outfitters). They donate 1 percent of their sales to groups working to ensure we have a habitable planet for people and fish. Temple Fork Outfitters donates $10 from the sale of each tenkara rod to various fishery environmental causes.